The Home Business Owners Start-up Guide

A 7-step process to formulate the Plan for your Business

BY

A.K. ANTHONY

Copyright © 2019

All Rights Reserved. No part of this publication may be reproduced in any form or by any means, including scanning, photocopying, or otherwise without prior written permission of the copyright holder.

ISBN Number: 9781677054152

Income Disclaimer

This Guide contains business start-up strategies, marketing methods, and other business advice that, regardless of my own results and experience, may not produce the same results [or any results] for you. I make absolutely no guarantee, expressed or implied, that by following the advice below you will make any money or improve current profits, as there are several factors and variables that come into play regarding any given business.

Primarily, results will depend on the nature of the product or business model, the conditions of the marketplace, the experience of the individual, and situations and elements that are beyond my control.

As with any business endeavor, you assume all risk related to investment and money based on your own discretion and at your own potential expense.

Liability Disclaimer

By reading this Guide, you assume all risks associated with using the advice given therein, with a full understanding that you, solely, are responsible for anything that may occur as a result of putting this information into action in any way, and regardless of your interpretation of the advice.

You further agree that I, or my successors and assigns, cannot be held responsible in any way for the success or failure of your business as a result of the information presented in this Guide. It is your responsibility to conduct your own due diligence regarding the safe and successful operation of your business if you intend to apply any of my information in any way to your business operations.

Terms of Use

You are given a non-transferable, "personal use" license to this Guide. You cannot distribute it or share it with other individuals.

Also, there are no resale rights or private label rights granted when purchasing this Guide. In other words, it's for your own personal use only.

TABLE OF CONTENTS

WHAT IS THE GUIDE ABOUT? 1

PART 1 - IS BEING A HOME BUSINESS OWNER REALLY WHAT I WANT TO DO? 9

WHERE DO I START? 10

MY OWN VENTURE INTO BUSINESS OWNERSHIP 17

SO, YOU WANT TO START YOUR OWN HOME BUSINESS. ... 25

SO WHY DO PEOPLE START THEIR OWN HOME BUSINESS? 27

LEVERAGING THE BEST OF YOU 38

WHAT TYPE OF BUSINESS WILL I HAVE? 45

FORMING YOUR COMPANY 59

INTELLECTUAL PROPERTY, TRADEMARKS, COPYRIGHT & PATENTS 66

TO SUMMARIZE 72

PART 2 - THE FIRST 6 STEPS IN THE PROCESS 74

INTRODUCTION 75

PLANNING YOUR BUSINESS 80

STEP 1 - DEFINING THE BUSINESS 84

START-UP RESOURCES 88

STEP 2 – THE PRODUCT 91

STEP 3 – THE MARKETING PLAN 104

- **STEP 4 - THE GROWTH PLAN** 122
- **STEP 5 – THE FINANCIAL PLAN** 139
- **STEP 6 – AN ANALYSIS OF THE BUSINESS** 172
- **PART 3 - STEP 7 - FINDING AND WORKING WITH A MENTOR** 178
- **INTRODUCTION TO MENTORING** 179
- **PART 3.1 - WHAT IS MENTORING?** 181
- **FORMS OR TYPES OF MENTORING** 185
- **WHO ARE MENTORS AND HOW CAN THEY HELP ME?** 190
- **MENTORING VERSUS OTHER FORMS OF TRAINING** 197
- **PART 3.2 - HOW TO BE MENTORED** 201
- **PREPARING FOR THE PROCESS** 206
- **FINDING AND DECIDING ON A MENTOR** 209
- **FORMALISING THE ARRANGEMENT** 223
- **HOW THE PROCESS WILL WORK** 229
- **ENDING THE RELATIONSHIP** 233
- **LAUNCH DAY** 237

AK ANTHONY

What is the Guide about?
The shorter the book, the less the bullshit
Stephen King - On Writing

Thank you for taking the time to read this Guide and I hope that you will find it an enjoyable and informative read.

Starting your own business is both frightening and exhilarating. It will take you through an endless roller coaster of highs, and lows that you can only imagine at this stage. But remember: the journey can be as fulfilling as the outcome.

Whether you are answering a lifelong passion to own your own business or turning a hobby into a paying venture or looking to establish a part-time interest to make some extra cash to cover the bills, the start-up requirements will be the same and as with any new undertaking, failure should not be an option.

I believe that if you spend the time and effort in laying the foundation for a new business then you need to be tooled up to take it from concept to fruition—if you take on a project of this nature then doing it the right way is the only way.

Unlike other business operations, the home business owner faces a unique challenge - they conduct the entire business daily in the building the rest of the family call "home". This means the family will be exposed to the various aspects of the business whether directly or indirectly. There is no escaping to the other office for the owner when family pressures mount. It is "one for all and all for one".

You are encouraged, in the first portion of this Guide to pause your dream for a moment and to think long and hard about what it is you are hoping to achieve: is your head in the right space, do you know what type of business you will launch, are your financial ducks in a row and is the family behind you?

Owning a business is not for everyone, and nor should it be. The traits and characteristics that may help someone turn an idea into a financially viable business opportunity are no more special than the traits and characteristics displayed by successful CEO's, Divisional Managers, Junior Line Managers and many employees in large corporations or Public service.

It comes down to an emotional or mental state that says, "this is right for me".

We will explore your idea or concept of being a home business owner. Is this a genuine desire or a passing fad? What are your goals and what is the underlining reason for taking such a life-changing decision? Do you have the commitment and determination, and yes, the passion, to make your idea a reality?

This Guide is a journey of questions, that you, as a prospective home business owner need to answer. It is a self-evaluation of whether this choice is the right fit, but it will underline the fact that anyone, irrespective of skill level, background or experience, can, if the commitment and determination to succeed are there, start their own business.

The statistics tell us that on average 80% of all new small businesses will fail in the first 12 to 18 months, my aim with Guide is to help you minimize your chances of becoming just another failed start-up.

The Home Business Owners Start-up Guide will take you through the entire process for starting your own home-based business, from concept to launch.

WHO SHOULD READ THE GUIDE?

The Guide is aimed at those who:

- are considering starting their own home-based business;
- have recently launched a business and are still within those worrisome first 12 to 18 months, or;
- are first time entrepreneurs, been in business for a while and feel it is time to re-test the business plan and growth strategies.

The Guide is structured in such a way that it will allow you to plug into a section or chapter that could specifically interest you and will speak to the issues or problems that you believe need a revisit.

WHAT QUALIFIES ME TO WRITE THIS GUIDE?

The answer: many years of trials, tribulations, successes and failures as a small and home-based business owner and in the first part of the Guide, I will share some of my journey with you in more detail.

If you are wondering why I have devoted all this time and effort in compiling the Guide, it is because I believe that in today's economic climate with the ongoing layoffs of employees and the growing concern that job security is no longer a right, privilege or a given, the number of home-based business start-ups will continue to increase. More and more unemployed, destitute families will look to innovative ways to provide for their loved ones. I hope, through this Guide to offer structured, simplistic and low-cost options for starting a home-based business.

It will not be easy, and time, effort and commitment are required. As Estee Lauder put it:

> *"I never dreamed about success. I worked for it."*

THE STRUCTURE OF THE GUIDE

As with any new project or undertaking, launched with the prospect of success in mind, planning is a natural first step, and so it is with starting a new home-based business.

The experts tell us that 80% of all new home and small business start-ups will fail in the first 12 to 18 months of operation. But just because successful entrepreneurs such as Sir Richard Branson, Bill Gates, Steve Jobs, Walt Disney, Oprah Winfrey, and Henry Ford, just to name a few, failed in their first business endeavors, it is not a requirement that you need to emulate them. There is no good reason for you to start your entrepreneurial journey with the impression that you will probably fail the first time around. Conversely, it would be naïve to assume that you are immune to failing but it is important that the thoughts of possible failure do not retard your positive attitude and become the impediment that stops you from trying to achieve your goals. Failure from time to time affects all of us and there will be times when bad decisions or lack of foresight will result in plans going south, as they sometimes have a tendency to do, but these mistakes or failures are not necessarily terminal for the business. Learn from the mistakes. Getting knocked down is just part of life, but it's how you get back up and deal with the setbacks that will distinguish you from the herd. Get that failure monkey off your back as soon as you can! I will be talking more about dealing with your fears later.

I have experienced the demoralizing and emotionally devastating fallout brought about through failure and, as a mentor or coach, I have helped several homes and small business owners return from the brink of failure. I am of the firm opinion that a primary reason business fail is they run out of money and they run out of money because they did not develop a detailed, viable and actionable plan for their business at the outset.

It is for this reason that a substantial amount of space in this Guide is dedicated to the formulation of your business plan.

Whether you use a professional to compile a formal Business Plan or you construct your own less formal document, a sound plan is a foundation for any successful venture. I have avoided any attempts to spoon feed you as the reader, rather I have laid out the guidelines to accomplish each step in the process hoping you will accept the challenge and go out there and do the research and investigation. It is your business and your future at stake here, so either I can share with you a step-by-step idiots guide on how you should proceed or, I can give you enough information to steer you in the right direction and believe that your innovative and inquisitive nature and your determination to succeed, will see you over the finish line. I have opted for the latter.

> *"Spoon feeding, in the long run, teaches us nothing but the shape of the spoon." E. M. Forster*

As with every new project or venture, there is a process, taking you from the start point, usually an idea or concept, through the research, evaluation and creation and finally to implementation. A simple 1-2-3 formula. Starting your own business is no different. To simplify the 3-part formula, I have broken down the process of creating your own home-based business into a preamble and 7 steps.

THE HOME BUSINESS OWNERS START-UP GUIDE

Preamble:	Self-evaluation
	Deciding on the type of business you will launch and establishing the Company
Step 1	Defining the Business
Step 2	The Product
Step 3	The Marketing Plan
Step 4	The Growth Plan
Step 5	The Financial Plan
Step 6	Business Analysis
Step 7	Finding and working with a mentor

For ease of use the Guide is broken up into three distinct parts.

PART 1

The Guide starts with some introspection, an evaluation of your decision to become a business owner, and the implications of your decision.

- Self-evaluation – is being a business owner what I want to do?
- Deciding on the type of business you will launch and establishing the Company.

Including the formation of the company, defining its broad purpose and followed by a discussion about the different company structures, the legal aspects, what you will need to get started and how to keep a close administrative eye on the business. We will also consider the start-up requirements for the business.

However, before we begin to formulate your business idea, I have included a chapter in this Part 1 in which I share my own experiences in business ownership. My hope is that this personal interlude will serve as a template against which you are able to measure your own progress and successes

PART 2

- Defining the Business, the Product, penetrating the market and preparing the way for future growth [Steps 1,2, 3 and 4]

In Part 2, we will begin with deciding upon and then defining the product your business will offer to the market place. Now that you know what your company will look like and the product or service you will sell, it will be necessary to detail the processes you will need to implement to announce your arrival – your Marketing Plan. Although it may appear to be premature, it is important to plan for the future growth of the company. If you don't know where you are going, you won't know how to get there. This is the Growth Plan

- Funding the venture and Analyzing the Plan [Steps 5 and 6]

To complete your business plan, you must understand the financial implications – have you saved up enough or will you need to borrow? An analysis of the business will follow identifying perceived strengths and weaknesses.

PART 3

- The final part of this Guide will show you how to find a mentor and what as the mentee, you should focus on during the relationship (Step 7), and ends with getting the business launched, yes, the day has arrived.

What this Guide is NOT ABOUT.

If a Plumbing business is what you're about, you will not find any information about how to fix geysers or toilets in this Guide.

Similarly, if selling goods through an online website is your chosen profession, I assume you have done all the necessary homework on how to build a website and display your product range.

As you make your way through the Guide, you will notice that words and phrases such as "research", "investigation", "planning" and "involve the family" are repeated, almost to the point of annoyance. This is deliberate, and I make no apologies. The intention is to encourage you to include these words into your everyday vocabulary for your business.

As you start out on your home business journey and take your bathtub dream to a reality, allow me to share the thoughts of someone who indirectly has positively influenced my own life, Nelson Mandela, who said

> *"There is no passion to be found playing small -*
> *in settling for a life that is less than the one you*
> *are capable of living."*

PART 1 - Is being a home business owner really what I want to do?

Where do I start?

"If you can dream it, you can do it."
Walt Disney

The first thing I would encouraging you to do is to pause for a moment and evaluate your intentions, asking those difficult questions that should help you decide if business ownership is for you.

I will explore the reasons why folks opt to own their own business with the risks, stress and rewards that business ownership entails as opposed to the security provided by being employed in the corporate world.

It is my intention that by the end of this chapter you will get a clear perception of what lies ahead in your entrepreneurial journey and what is expected of you in terms of effort, commitment and time. You will have considered the risks involved and whether you and your loved ones are in the right space and frame of mind to take the leap of faith.

It is important to understand that unless you are looking to generate extra cash by turning your hobby into a part-time business of sorts, starting your own business is not some short-term experiment. If you intend to make a sustainable success of your business, you need to appreciate that you are in it for the long haul.

Do you qualify to be a home business owner? I don't know, only you can answer that, but my intention is to explore the various aspects of what might influence your decision. I do not intend to pressure you either way but only to lay before you the issues you need to consider. As you reach the end, you will have been given enough information to decide whether being an entrepreneur is what you want to be.

As you will discover, I am not a believer in the theory that only a "special breed" of people succeed as business owners. I certainly do not have a third eye or Jedi like skills or talents.

Everyday folks like you and I have, most times, surpassed all expectations of others and even themselves, and taken their dreams from street corners, tin shacks, garages, kitchens and back rooms, and converted them into profitable, sustainable and growing businesses and even sometimes, launched brands that have become household names.

Here are examples of famous brands that started in someone's home:

Amazon
Apple
Disney
Google
Harley Davidson
Hewlett-Packard
Lotus Cars
Maglite
Mattel
Yankee Candle Company

The list is provided courtesy of www. retireat21.com

BEFORE YOU START

Many aspirant home business entrepreneurs quickly find that, although they have an intimate knowledge of the proposed product or service they intend to sell, they are lacking in certain business-related skills or expertize. Understandable and no need for panic.

In fact, the sooner you acknowledge your shortcomings, the sooner you will remedy them. If needed get external help and never be reluctant or embarrassed to ask for help when necessary.

I am not the sole source for starting a home or small business. Although it is possible to over analyze the process, don't hesitate to seek a second or even a third opinion from other mentors or start-up experts if it makes you feel more comfortable.

Just don't procrastinate to avoid taking the next step.

You may gather as you work your way through the Guide, that I am not a qualified accountant or lawyer. My financial and legal knowledge, although still somewhat limited was learned during my years as a small business owner leaning on the ability of others and on whom I continuously rely.

It is for this reason that I will constantly refer you to professional sources whenever I believe that my knowledge or experience is not adequate to provide you with the correct or complete information that I consider you need, for a specific topic.

It is probable that, unless you are qualified in one of these areas, financial and legal help is what you will need in the early stages of starting up your business. I also recommend that you look for an experienced business mentor even if it is only to have someone who has been there, to bounce ideas off. I am a fanatic in recommending that ALL new entrepreneurs find a mentor to guide them through the start-up phase of the business.

I will continue to highlight the benefits of having a mentor for your start-up from time to time throughout the Guide, hoping you will heed my advice. It has been my good fortune to receive mentoring on and off during my entire working career thus enabling me to reciprocate my good fortune by mentoring new entrepreneurs. As an added bonus mentors will usually not charge for their services. Part 3 of this Guide is dedicated to helping you source and work with mentors.

"If you cannot see where you are going, ask someone who has been there before."

- J. Loren Norris

The Internet, as with libraries [those big buildings with lots of books in them], can offer a wealth of free information. I built my web sites on my own [super proud I was] using a product called WordPress, and everything I needed to know I gleaned from videos on YouTube, the WordPress Technical forums and helpful articles on web sites.

However, a word of caution: the adage "you can't believe everything you see on TV" applies in bucket loads with the Internet. Verify your information; if you are using sites like Forbes or Entrepreneur.com, you can rest assured the guidance provided is substantiated and legitimate. An advert or article proclaiming that "in exchange for $5000 I will make you a millionaire in a day" needs serious investigation before signing up.

Being a "Jack of all trades" implies a "master of none". Concentrate on what you excel at and become the very best you can be in your chosen profession and leave what is not your "cup of tea" to those with the requisite skills and expertize.

I hope this interlude has been helpful, but let's now turn our attention to talking about home business ownership, beginning with a brief explanation of what a home business is.

What constitutes a home-based business?

Let's begin with some background information into what is a home or small business.

The definition of a SMALL business depends on the country in which it is being defined. In the US, it is a company with fewer than 250 employees, in Australia fewer than 15 employees and in the European Union, it is defined as a company with less than 50 employees.

In my country South Africa, the National Small Business Act uses the acronym SMME, for SMALL, MICRO and MEDIUM Enterprises to group the various smaller entities together.

The MICRO is defined as having less than 5 employees and family-owned - otherwise known as a home-based business. It further divides small into SMALL and VERY SMALL enterprises with less than 100 and less than 10 employees, respectively.

Oddly enough, it classifies Micro as part of *the informal business sector*. This may have to do with the fact that the vast majority of these types of business have, in the past, operated in rural areas and townships and did so without formal company registration. This is changing.

So, what classifies a small business as a "home" business?

WIKIPEDIA defines HOME BUSINESS as

"A home business [or "home-based business" or "HBB"] is a small business that operates from the business owner's home office. In addition to location, home businesses are usually defined by having a very small number of employees, usually all immediate family of the business owner, in which case it is also a family business. Home businesses generally lack shop frontage, customer

parking and street advertising signs. Such businesses are sometimes prohibited by residential zoning regulations."

Wikipedia also goes onto to say, *"The concept of home-based business, as opposed to the previous terminology of "cottage industry", first appeared in 1978. The phrase was coined by Marion Behr, the originator of a study to find out what businesses women throughout America were carrying on in their homes"*

By definition, the home-based business is just that. It means that all the activities associated with your business are performed at your place of residence, unless you provide a service, such as plumbing, and therefore you are also out at other people's premises.

For me, a SMALL business implies a company with a limited number of employees but operates from purchased or rented premises, for example, a suite of offices or warehouse. The scope and/or size of the operation prevents it from operating from a place of residence.

Referring to yourself as a home-based business and working from home just because you don't enjoy working from your company offices or warehouse is semantics.

The focus of this Guide is on the HOME-BASED BUSINESS OWNER, although much of the content also applies to a SMALL business owner.

SOME FACTS ABOUT SMALL AND HOME BUSINESS

For many economies around the world, the small and home-based business sector is viewed as the forefront of the economy. Some countries view the strength of the small business environment as an indicator of the overall strength of their economy. Possibly due to the impact of periodic downturns in the global economy and the resultant increase in unemployment, the home business sector continues to grow.

Before we get started here are some interesting facts about Home and Small business.

On average, a new home-based business is started every 12 seconds.

There are just under 40 million home-based businesses in the US [at the time of writing].

According to the 2012 Global Entrepreneurship Monitor report, home businesses start up with under $15,000. Most start-ups are self-funded, or by friends or family.

70% of all Americans confessed to wanting to be self-employed. 69% of US entrepreneurs started their businesses from home.

Women are considered being more likely to succeed with a home business than men.

Ownership does not have any age patterns

With the advent of "virtual employees and virtual offices", home-based businesses can expand much quicker and at lower input costs.

My own venture into business ownership

The purpose of sharing my own entrepreneurial journey is not an attempt to write a memoir that would probably bore you to tears. It is more about highlighting what worked and what failed, so you, the entrepreneur or prospective business owner, better understand the realities of starting and owning your own business. Each of the lessons I learned along the way has been marked [lesson #] and summarized at the end of the chapter–a cheat sheet if you like.

If you take nothing else away from this Guide but these 6 lessons, then my work here is done, as they say in the classics.

The knowledge and information shared in this Guide is not a compilation of examples taken from other practitioners' books and articles, but is drawn from my personal experiences, and those of others, with whom I have had the pleasure and honor of sharing in their entrepreneurial journey and reflects the realities of life as a home business owner.

AND SO HERE IS A SYNOPSIS OF MY EARLY BUSINESS CAREER.

After spending almost 9 years in uniform and with no commercial qualification or experience, I took my first tentative steps into the rather intimidating world of corporate employment. I must admit that from the outset, I found the experience mundane and not exciting but lacking in any academic qualification, I was forced to accept positions not out of choice but from necessity. Despite this, I did manage to carve out a reasonable career in the supply chain management function, eventually reaching the dizzy heights [for me anyway] of middle management.

One benefit of working within this commercially orientated function was that it allowed me to interact with not only large company sales folks but more influentially, I began to meet business people who owned their own small businesses. I became intrigued by the unique challenges they faced and the appearance of being "in control" of their future. Owning your own business seemed like a lot of fun and richly rewarding.

After enduring the corporate life [and no, I am not knocking corporate folks, it was just not for me] for just short of 16 years, I was certain I had accumulated sufficient experience and expertize to go it alone and so about 15 years ago I ventured out into the big wide world of business ownership.

With disastrous results.

Despite my unshakeable belief that I could make large amounts of money in no time at all, working hours of my choosing and defining my sun-blessed future, I discovered to my dismay that I was ill-equipped, self-opinionated and lacking in even the most basic skills necessary to start a company, never mind sustaining one.

In a very short space of time my total disregard for the very fundamentals of entrepreneurship: doing the necessary research, planning and above all LISTENING to others who had trodden the same path, quickly brought about my demise as a business owner. Not only was I successful at failing once, but I achieved the distinction of recording a string of embarrassing failures, placing my family in a financial crisis and falling very short of securing "financial freedom" and so-called "control over my destiny". [Lesson #1: don't go jumping into deep water unless you can swim!]

A very bitter pill to swallow. Talk about ego crushing.

A short stint back in corporate "uniform" gave me the time to recover financially and ponder my mistakes–what had I done, or not done, that caused me to fail?

MY RE-EVALUATION

My point of departure during this period of introspection was understanding WHY. Why did I want to own a business considering the risk and the turmoil I had experienced during my first outings?

Understanding the why was difficult to grasp. I no longer subscribed to the "I want to be my own boss" and "I want financial freedom" mantra's anymore because I understood that to me, they were a glib collective for "I hate my job" and did not deal with the WHY I want my own business.

After many hours of deep meditation [which sometimes meant just staring out into space with nothing intelligent on the mind] and some serious soul searching, I came to the belief that my real motivating reasons for wanting to create my own business were threefold.

First, to secure financial stability. Note, not freedom or "I want to be rich", but stability.

Secondly, to provide a viable and going concern which could be left to my children, should they wish it, or at least to ensure financial support until they could launch their own careers. A personal legacy if you like.

Thirdly, to pursue, with enthusiasm and commitment and without restrictions, ideas and concepts that I believed in. Ideas that applied to an industry or working environment that I was comfortable with and in which I could achieve control over my decision-making processes.

Acknowledging the WHY made it a lot easier to plan the next steps. [Lesson #2: understand why you want to be a business owner]

The first of which was to decide on what type of business did I want to do. On first entering the realm of business ownership, I followed the advice of many so-called gurus and "followed my passions", "do what you love and love what you do" sounded so plausible to me and appeared to provide the link to my dreams of what I would look like after clocking up my first world-shaking success. I wanted to wake up every morning all fired up and go off to work to do something I was passionate about, not the boring stuff I had done in the corporate world.

The reality was that although I was passionate about the early choices I had made about the type of business I was launching, I lacked the skill and experience to turn my passions into moneymaking operations. No matter how passionate I was, trying to learn about the product or service I wanted to sell while simultaneously starting the company was a recipe for failure.

These experiences clarified that being passionate about something was not enough when it came to decide on a business type and was not enough to make the business a success. There had to be more depth to the decision. I had to be looking at ventures that provided me with a saleable product about which I had more than just cursory knowledge. [Lesson #3: passion alone does not guarantee success]

Enter stage left: my first business mentor.

I approached a long-time friend who also was a very successful small business owner with the question—so what should I do? And got the best business advice I had received to date. In a no-nonsense, straight to the point and rather blunt way [which mentors do] he told me to "forget all this passion crap you have read about and look at what you do well." Unfortunately, for me, the only thing I knew how to do when it came to business was what I had been doing for so many years in the corporate environment—and had hated with a "passion".

Although my immediate reaction was something like "not in my lifetime", the more I thought about it the more sense it made. Although not to my liking I had to admit that it was something for which I was trained and according to my various previous bosses, good at. There was a ready market, and I already knew many of the potential customers.

Problem solved: I knew what it was I would do. [Lesson #4]

On the advice of my newfound mentor, [he didn't know at the time that I had decided he had become my support pillar] I began to talk to other people who owned their own businesses to hear first-hand their experiences. It helped me learn what worked and what didn't and saved me an awful amount of time—I wasn't reinventing the wheel. I read a lot about why some succeed, and others fail. I expanded my personal network, and I learned how to LISTEN. All the smart people I know are great listeners and when they share information, it is worth taking the time to focus and take copious notes. [Lesson #5: learn to listen!]

This led me to a new set of questions.

- Did I have what it takes to go it alone?
- What was it I needed to go it alone?
- Was success guaranteed?
- Did I understand the business environment?

- Could I achieve my goals without placing my family at risk?

Many of these could not be answered with a simple yes or no and in some cases, only time would provide the answer but I did feel confident enough to launch and after a very difficult 3 years, I was able to invest the proceeds of my first successful launch into other projects of a more interesting nature.

Having to start a business doing something that is not your first choice is difficult. It took an enormous amount of will power and determination to make it work but the most worrying factor for me at the outset [other than my lack of passion], was whether I could convince a customer I had a product to sell and that I was competent enough to meet his or her performance criteria. This turned out to be of little consequence—the corporate experience had taught me well. [Lesson #6: look to your experiences]

LESSONS LEARNED

So why was I able to succeed this time around?

I had taken the time to learn what was needed to start and run a small business. I discovered that it was not a part-time exercise—it took total commitment.

Lesson #1—I needed to prepare. I had spent a lot of time on research and planning before I ventured into ownership. Preparation made the launch almost problem free and allowed me to concentrate from day one on getting my first customer under the belt. The market knew I was coming, and I knew what I had to offer.

Lesson #2—I had identified why I wanted to be an entrepreneur and more importantly, what I was hoping to achieve in the long term—financial stability and an improved [and secured] lifestyle for my family. No fantasies about financial freedom, living my dream, being my own boss and doing what I liked—just simple hard work.

Lesson #3—Although there were many things I was passionate about I had to put them aside as it was abundantly clear I did not have the skills or expertize to turn these personal passions into money-making opportunities. Passion alone does not guarantee success.

Lesson #4—My business model was based around what I knew I could do well and therefore could turn into a viable business.

Lesson #5—I learned how to listen and not to be afraid of asking for help when needed. My acknowledgment that yes, there are smarter people than me, helped me overcome my bias towards other success stories. Admitting I had failed, and therefore needed whatever help I could get, was of huge value to me.

I accepted that I was the average in "average Joe" and so needed the skills and expertize of others from time to time to ensure that my goals would be met. Learning from others going forward was just part of being a business owner. Which also substantiates my belief that anyone can be a business owner if he or she is determined enough to make it work.

Lesson #6—By accepting the advice of my first mentor and drawing on what life had taught me so far allowed me to overcome my distaste of having to go back to what I had been doing in the corporate world. Using all the skills and experiences gained during those years as an employee, was my lifesaver.

ADDITIONAL INSIGHTS

- I started out with the right mindset. The only thing I attempted to plan for with my first venture was what I would do if I failed. Having the mindset, even if only subconsciously, that failure is acceptable is fatal. This time around, failure was not even on the "what if" list. My mental focus was on success ONLY.

- It was apparent that having a financial reserve was critical, not only to finance the business but also to meet the needs of the household and family. I made sure there was sufficient in the piggy bank that would allow me to operate for at least six months without having to borrow money or to tap into personal savings, draw against insurance policies or dip into the kid's educational fund.

- I resolved not to borrow money from others, especially friends and family. I continued being employed until I had enough savings to fund myself.

- Family support and involvement when relevant was fundamental to succeeding.

- Taking calculated risks from time to time, were a necessary part of business ownership. The key was learning to identify which risks were acceptable and which weren't. I acknowledged that this skill would develop over time and that in the interim I would rely on the advice of trusted associates.

- Nothing was cast in stone.

These criteria are the foundation requirements I now share with my clients. Being well prepared in all facets of business ownership before you start, is a cornerstone to ultimate success.

And if you are wondering how you will determine which the right questions are to ask mentors you have just answered your own question. The first question you need to be asking is, "What questions do I need to be asking?"

So, you want to start your own home business.

Remember that starting a home-based business is no different from starting any other type of business. The only real difference is that your office is in your home.

When first approached by prospective home business owners, I ask them WHY they want to start their own business. The following tale may help explain why I believe this question has relevance and the reason it is so important to put serious thought to what you are contemplating.

Some time ago I met an ex-colleague from my corporate days for a drink in a hotel lounge where he was bemoaning his whole existence in general and his job at a large mining company in particular. The rest of the conversation went something like this:

HIM: "I hate my job. I do the same thing day in, day out. My boss doesn't understand me and doesn't realize how talented and smart I am. My staff are idiots and don't want to learn. I think I will start my own business."

ME: "Why?"

HIM: "Well, you know, I can do my own thing when I want, go where I want and make lots of money."

ME: "How do you know that?"

HIM: "Everyone knows that. I will be great working for myself, I just need to decide what I will do. I can make lots of money having my own business."

ME: "OK, let me put this another way—WHY?"

HIM: "I've just explained it. Man, you're just as stupid as my boss."

He then got up and left leaving me to pick up the tab.

Being a home business owner is a lifestyle that suits some more than others and is not for everyone. Choosing not to own your own business has nothing to do with a lack of commitment, passion, skill or fear of hard work. Working in the corporate environment can be just as challenging and rewarding and if you are one of those hardworking, happy, and content corporate folks, STAY WHERE YOU ARE. The small business owners appreciate your efforts.

So why do people start their own home business?

What makes some people decide to go it alone? What dynamic drives an individual to step out into the unknown and unleash his or her talents on an unsuspecting public?

Other than those folks who like myself just do not fit into the corporate world and yearn to influence their decision-making capabilities as it affects their livelihood, there are possibly 4 other reasons folks start their own business, but if you do not see yourself in any of these groupings don't stress, it doesn't mean you are atypical.

THE FIRST IS NECESSITY

I attribute necessity to several things, losing your job is the first one that comes to mind and is a cause that grows exponentially every time there is a financial fallout in our respective economies. Going into business because of forced circumstances is not ideal and quite often the start-up is unplanned, which leads to an early demise of the business.

The first challenge that arises is "What business am I going to do?" If you do not have a hobby, hidden talent or skill or other activity that you can turn into a business you will need to fall back on what you know best, which is not a bad option.

And what you know best probably relates to your most previous job [as in my story] but assumes that whatever you were doing is, in one form or another, saleable. One issue that rears its ugly head in this scenario is that if you were laid off in unpleasant circumstances [which I was not], you may not have a warm disposition towards doing anything that vaguely resembles your last job.

In addition, there is the not so small matter of getting fired up and passionate about what you are endeavoring to undertake. You're devastated by what has happened to you and the family is in a state of shock. It will be difficult to pull yourself up by the bootstraps and be upbeat. A whole heap of courage and determination is required and getting some outside help, be it from a mentor, a family member or an ex-colleague may be a good idea in the early stages. Positive thinking is the name of the game.

Alternatively, if you have something else you can turn to that takes you away from your past work environment, all the better.

THE SECOND IS A PERSONAL PASSION

How many times have you heard stories of stay at home moms [or dad's] who have turned a personal passion, for example, baking or repairing vehicles, into a lucrative home-based business? Plenty of times I'm sure, and the reason for that is that it often happens.

In my experience [which is miniscule in the greater scheme of things], I have found that most times the individual pursues the passion BEFORE it becomes a business. They do what they do because they love it and then someone says "Hey! Why aren't you making money from it?". Passion, in this instance, customarily comes along with a very generous helping of skill and creativity; people have been able to turn their creativity, personal talent, hobby, lifetime experiences or specific product knowledge into very successful home businesses. The primary driving force may be their passion, but it is underpinned by their extraordinary level of expertize. For example, cooking is the love of their lives and they are also very good at it.

You've already answered the big question as to what the business should look like and all the passion, skill, and expertize required to launch quickly is entrenched. Adding the finer points of business management is all that is needed.

However, a word of warning. I have also witnessed several businesses collapse because of the person relying on their passion, gift or skill and ignoring even the most basic principles of sound business management in their haste to launch. Passion alone is no guarantee of success!

THE THIRD GROUP IS THOSE WHO SPOT A UNIQUE OPPORTUNITY.

This is perhaps the smallest group but there are enough examples of this category around, so I won't bore you with a long list of success stories, but of course, Facebook and Apple are pertinent examples.

Spotting a unique opportunity is just the start. A solution, in the form of a product or service, must be developed to fill the gap. Great ideas sometimes require great funding and for the proposed solution to materialize a large corporate player or investor may be needed. The downside is large funders will probably want to either purchase your idea outright or absorb it into a larger structure. But if the idea is a winner—who cares.

THE FINAL GROUP IS THOSE WHO ARE JUST BORN ENTREPRENEURS

Everything they touch turns to gold - believe it or not, they do exist. In all likelihood their entrepreneurial careers started when they were still in nappies, conning their baby siblings into handing over their toys through masterful negotiation or with promises of profitable future joint ventures.

No, they are not perfect and make mistakes, fail and even go out of business on occasions, but they seem to have the knack of turning the simplest of ideas into multimillion-dollar enterprises. I have only met a few in my career but I acknowledge they are a pleasure to behold when in full flight. Don't despair if you do not fall into this category, there is plenty of room in the world of small business ownership for us mere mortals.

It is also worth mentioning 2 other scenarios which fall outside of the 4 above.

- People who don't like people or who do like people

One advantage of having an online business is that you don't have to deal face to face with people. So, if you have introvert tendencies operating your own business from the comfort and solace of your bedroom could be just the thing for you. Conversely, if helping others is your goal in life, then there are many opportunities to turn this "good guy" trait into money.

- The part-timer

The way some folks start out and it is an option worth considering if start-up funding is a problem. What makes this option attractive is that it ensures that the regular monthly income is still available while you launch your new home-based business. It is worthwhile checking on your conditions of employment if you go this route as some companies prohibit moonlighting. This is also a way to supplement the family income and there are many households where one or more of the members run small part-time business operations while being full-time employees and are content with their lot and do not intend to change it.

DO I NEED TO POSSESS SPECIAL TRAITS AND ATTRIBUTES?

So, do you have to be a special individual to start your own business or to achieve success? Are successful owners an extraordinary breed of people with unique skills and attributes?

I don't think so.

Having read numerous books on the subject and visited an untold number of "guru" web sites I am led to believe that without at least a substantial number of very special traits or characteristics you will fail.

Here is a list [extracted from various articles and posts on the subject] of some examples of what these *super beings* allegedly possess–

Passionate beyond normal expectations
Committed
Strive for business success above all else, even family
Never take leisure time or vacations
Ruthless
Visionaries
Inordinate risk takers–even at the expense of others
Exceptional leaders
Intolerant of mistakes
Strive to get everything right, first time
Arrogant and aggressive in all their business dealings
Prefer their own company–loners
Hands-on achievers
Want success at all costs
Idolized and emulated by subordinates
Outspoken and an expert in their field
Team Leaders… and the list goes on.

Wow!

Does this mean that if you cannot claim ownership to a good helping of these traits and attributes, you won't succeed as a home business owner? Are having these special traits or attributes a prerequisite to success?

I don't believe that to be true and permit me to explain why.

After many years of being in business, I have not as yet had the fortune to meet any one business owner or leader who can claim to possess all or most of these wonderful traits.

While some business owners possess certain personal attributes that contribute towards their success and the legends of the corporate business world certainly have something which sets them apart, we can't all be Sir Richard Branson, Bill Gates or Mark Zuckerberg. But we can achieve a level of success with our own God-given talents and be content with it.

I have met and worked with some very passionate and talented corporate folks at all levels who possess a good portion of the traits and attributes listed above. They love and thrive on what they do and experience in the corporate business environment and have no wish or desire to be a business owner.

I have friends, associates and clients that come from all walks of life who are owners of very successful home and small businesses and by their own admissions, do not possess any specialized skill sets or talents that make them <u>unique</u>. That does not mean that they are not talented, but not in a way that makes them members of a <u>unique business owners only club.</u>

There does not appear to be any scientific studies that point to a specific grouping of individuals or to a list of personal traits or attributes needed to be a successful entrepreneur. This would imply that there is not a "one fits all" description of what makes up a successful business owner.

A respected local entrepreneur and a colleague of mine had the pleasure of working with some young folk who come from our previously disadvantaged communities. Many of them did not complete their schooling, they have had no formal business training and the words marketing and business plans are not in their vocabulary. Yet they have taken their sidewalk businesses to incredible heights. They can spot a potential customer in a crowd, they know when market trends will shift, and they regularly turn other people's trash into saleable products.

How are they able to do this in the face of unbelievable challenges and obstacles that most entrepreneurs in the developed world have never even heard of? Here are some examples of the difficulties they face when starting out:

- bad locations—many do not have premises from which to market their wares;
- language barriers [there are 11 official languages in my country];
- no funding of any kind;
- no marketing or advertising training or tools, other than word of mouth or through their happy customers;
- no formal support from business chambers or associations, and;
- no form of transport, other than public transport, to increase their visibility.

So how do they succeed?

Certainly not from any formal education or training. Do they possess any of the traits listed above? Without question, but more importantly, they are street smart.

What, for me, stands out head and shoulders above all the theoretical reasons is:

- Their SELF CONFIDENCE, their unquestioned self-belief that they will succeed.

- TOTAL COMMITMENT to the endeavor–putting in the time and effort to make sure their business does not fail; working 18-hour days is not uncommon.

- Extensive knowledge of the market within which they operate, in other words their street smarts.

- UNDERSTANDING who the customer is and what they want: living in the same areas and continuously networking with their customers.

- EXPERT knowledge of their product or service: many of them are handmade.

All of which looks to me like a thorough understanding of the simple basics of business. Work hard, be committed and know your product and intended customer.

Sound like common sense?

We don't have to attend too many lectures or read a room full of business books to understand that successful enterprises come about because of a combination of factors as opposed to the single influence of a gifted or talented owner.

Having the right product in the right market, a well-managed financial model, trusted and committed employees and a logical and implementable marketing plan may also have something to do with it.

It's not only about how many personal traits and attributes a business owner may have; trying to sell ice to the folks in Alaska is likely to end in failure.

Companies don't fail solely because of a scarcity of any special attributes in the owner.

They go under because they run out of money brought about by various factors: a bad product mix, weak financial management and planning, and poor customer relations but sometimes caused by factors outside of their control, as we saw with the worldwide financial calamity in 2008.

SO WHY DO BUSINESSES FAIL?

I do not intend to devote much time to this depressing topic. Spending too much time pondering on what may go wrong and how to build in blocks and checks to ensure it won't happen, although necessary, is not what your primary focus should be.

According to Bloomberg, 8 out of 10 businesses will fail within the first 18 months of a start-up. What causes this alarming statistic, assuming it is correct and applicable to all countries and all industries?

As I have already said, in my humble opinion, businesses fail because they run out of money.

Unless income exceeds expenditure, the ultimate outcome will be a failure. What may contribute to this will become clearer as we move through each component of your business plan but here is a summarized version of some pitfalls to avoid.

Lack of start-up funding. This applies not only to the needs of your new business but also includes enough money to cover the family and household needs. I have always used a "rule of thumb" calculation which dictates that there must be enough cash in the piggy bank to provide cover for at least 6 months of operation, assuming a worst-case scenario of having made no sales in this period.

Lack of family support. I think I have covered this topic ad infinitum, but it can be a crippling factor. I know, as I speak from experience.

No plan. This Guide is all about constructing the business plan, so enough said for now.

The wrong product–Again, we will go into this in more detail but as you will have already read in this Guide–no product, or the wrong product, is a non-starter.

Getting the head right. If you intend to launch a business, it must be with total commitment and the right mindset [unless it is just a hobby or a fun thing to do]. Trying to launch with one foot in the new enterprise and the other in some other venture will result in you tripping over your shoelaces and landing on your face.

Lack of business skills. This will only become a problem if you do not take the time to assess your strengths and weaknesses and are too proud, or shy, to know when you need to ask for help. More about this as we move through the rest of the Guide.

IN SUMMARY:

Do I think you need to be a special breed of person or have unique traits and attributes?

NO!

Do I think you can sit back and wait for fortune and riches to fall into your lap?

Absolutely NOT!

Is success guaranteed?

NO. Being a home business owner will require lots of hard work, dedication, commitment, and innovative thinking.

Can anyone determined to make it work own a home-based business?

A resounding YES!

Leveraging the best of you

I have always assumed that the mark of a successful business is when it continues to make a profit. How it achieved this milestone could be a combination of different factors such as brilliant management, hardworking employees, a great strategy, the right product in the right market, sound financial planning, a clever marketing approach, good luck and a sprinkling of magic dust.

There are so many factors that will influence the performance of any company, irrespective of its size, and therefore trying to home in on one or more aspect that you believe will help you outpace your competitors, is at this early stage, difficult. What I believe you can do is look at those aspects that you have control over and understand how best to leverage your own strengths.

KNOW YOUR STRENGTHS AND WEAKNESSES.

Very early in my working career, I realized that there were certain business skills and personal traits I did not possess and was unlikely to possess anytime in the future. So where necessary I called on other more talented folks to help and learned what I could from them.

From my experience of mentoring and observing successful small and home business owners it is my humble opinion that even the most "average of Joe's" can become a successful business owner. You only need to acknowledge what you can do and what you can't and accept that you will from time to time need to enlist the help of those who are more skilled.

I recently met a very rich business owner, who started out as a home business owner, and now runs a group of tool and die manufacturing companies in three different countries. By his own admission, he is introvert, obnoxious, and dislikes people in general.

What, in his opinion, made him successful?

His personal drive to succeed at all costs and his ability to acknowledge his shortcomings.

From the outset, he employed people who could provide him with the skill sets he lacked, with particular emphasis on managing employees and dealing with customers.

Drawing up a list of our own strengths and weaknesses as we perceive them can be difficult and it is likely you will short-change yourself. The human tendency to be self-critical will result in your list of weaknesses far outnumbering your list of strengths.

So, to help with this exercise can I recommend you enlist the input of friends, colleagues [or ex-colleagues], relatives and anybody who knows you well. Approach folks who will be honest and not tell you what they think you want to hear.

Ask each one to draw up a list for you of what they recognize as your strengths and weaknesses—compare it to your own. This list highlights areas in which you will feel confident in managing and controlling.

For example, if one of your strengths is the ability to work with numbers, managing the financial aspects of your business is something to keep close to your chest, if numbers are not your thing then you will need a full-time accountant.

Conversely, not being comfortable around people may be a weakness that is flashing bright red lights at you suggesting that maybe an Internet-based business would be more suitable than trying to launch a Human Resource consulting company.

Get the idea?

This list will also be handy when we explore in the next part of this Guide, the type of business you should launch.

DEAL WITH THE FEAR OF FAILURE

As already mentioned, the statistics show that 80% of all new start-ups fail within the first 12 to 18 months, and if that doesn't put the fear of failure into you, nothing will.

I have already discussed some of the reasons new start-ups fail and more will become clear as we go through the Guide but the very first roadblock to success you are likely to encounter is YOU.

As you have heard frequently, there are no guarantees in life, and business start-ups fall very much into this description. You will probably have the odds stacked against you but unless you face up to this and find the best ways to deal with your fears, failure is the probable outcome.

As Nelson Mandela put it, *"It always seems impossible until it's done,"*

The first step in overcoming the potential roadblock of your fear of failure is to admit to it. If you are about to launch your very first business and you are not fearful, I would beg to question your understanding of what you are about to undertake. Fear of the unknown is just human nature—it is how you deal with it that will make the difference.

If you don't acknowledge your fear and the resultant cautiousness, you could succumb to the one thing that will definitely torpedo your dreams—procrastination.

There is a clear distinction between hesitation because you need to verify something and hesitation because you are too afraid to take the next step. Doing nothing can be a conscious decision to do so, but to do nothing to avoid deciding is inexcusable.

This may sound contradictory, but I recommend that you never lose sight of your fear of failing. Used correctly, it can become a motivator. As with all things in life failure brings consequences and knowing what the consequences of your business failing will be, both to you and your loved ones can be the very motivation that drives you to succeed.

As with any new venture being prepared to the very best of your ability is about the most proactive thing you can do. Here are some thoughts on what you can do now to help you manage those jitters.

As mentioned previously, know your STRENGTHS and WEAKNESSES.

PLANNING and RESEARCH are critical elements for any new start-up and the more detailed it is the better you will be able to "bob and weave" your way through the challenges and obstacles that the business world is going to throw at you. The more detailed your planning and research is BEFORE you launch the less likely the unexpected will ambush you.

Be prepared to LISTEN. Now is the time to start meeting and talking to business owners, listen to their experiences, and take to heart the gems that they will share with you. You don't have to know them, just pick up the phone and call several small businesses in your immediate area. I guarantee they will be happy to meet with you. Learn from those who have been there and done it.

Get your HEAD right. As I have mentioned before, going it alone is not something you do because you are bored at work. It is a permanent change in your lifestyle and that of your loved ones. Start thinking like a business owner NOW.

IMPROVE your SKILLS and KNOWLEDGE to the very best level that you can. Be confident about your expertize and in your own ability to achieve. No matter what you intend to do, there is every likelihood that someone, somewhere, at some time has already done it - so why can't you?

Focus on the rewards that will accrue to you and your loved ones when your business is rocketing along as opposed to all the bad things that might happen. Give yourself a great big "YES, I CAN DO IT" every time any doubt creeps in.

My most important recommendation?

Get used to the idea that you will need to ask for HELP from folks who are smarter than you. Start now by drawing up a list of folks who you think you would be comfortable approaching for help. Get talking to them as soon as you need to.

I came across this very quaint fable [by an anonymous author] which is so true to life:

A man was trying very hard to lift a large rock.
His friend approached and asked him, "Are you using all of your strength?"
"Yes, I'm trying my hardest," the man said.
"Are you sure?" the friend pressed him.
"Of course, I'm using all of my strength!" the man replied impatiently.
"No, you're not," said the friend. "I'm standing right here, and you haven't asked me for help."

Think about a MENTOR. Mentors are skilled, knowledgeable, and approachable people who have a wealth of expertize and experience that they are willing to share with folks like us.

And whatever you do remember there are family members or other loved ones that rely on you for one or more reasons—involve them from the get-go and keep them in the loop. If you have a family and you are the sole or main breadwinner think CAREFULLY about what you are intending to do and share every step of your thought processes with them constantly

And don't forget to listen to your GUT INSTINCTS!

TO SUMMARIZE

Great! You are still with me.

Let's look back at what we have covered:

You received a short history lesson about home businesses and some stats about them—interesting but the one fact you need to keep in mind is the failure rate.

I shared some of my own experiences with you not to convince you that this is the only way to get your business launched but more to highlight some erroneous steps I took that you might avoid.

We listed 4 main categories of why people start their own businesses and I did not include this to take up pages, but to encourage you to put some thought to the WHY you want to start your own enterprise. Understanding why it is you want to take this life-changing step is contributing a big chunk towards creating a solid foundation for your business.

Remember this quote from author Terry Pratchett

> *"If you do not know where you come from, then you don't know where you are, and if you don't know where you are, then you don't know where you're going. And if you don't know where you're going, you're probably going wrong."*

Do you, as a prospective home or small business owner, have to be a special person? I think we hit that perception on the head, not intending to undermine or diminish the talents or skills of others but to make you understand that with the right mindset, a winning attitude and the determination to put in the hard work, you too [with some help from this Guide] can be a successful home business owner.

In the last chapter, we looked at understanding your strengths and weaknesses and how to deal with your fears and trepidations and to use them as motivators as opposed to inhibitors.

Now that we've done all the introspection bit and you feel comfortable with your choice to be a successful home business owner let's get this business of yours off the ground.

What type of business will I have?

We discussed the various reasons some folks opt to start their own business venture as opposed to finding full-time employment in a company. I don't intend to revisit that discussion, so I will assume that you have already had your epiphany and have explored more earnestly the prospects of starting a home-based business.

Converting ideas and dreams into reality seem so simple when in your bath or with friends at the local pub. But the truth is, it can be a lot more tedious than one would expect. The reason is that if you are serious about turning your dream into a going concern; you need to do some serious homework, and I will show you how.

Let's get started with the fun stuff. Grab a pen and some paper and jot down these 4 questions.

1. What business am I going to start?
2. Can I do it from home?
3. Can I quit my job now or should I wait, and if so for how long?
4. What impact do I think it will have on the family/friends/loved ones?

Now go away and think about your answers and WRITE THEM DOWN on your piece of paper, bullets points are fine at this stage. We will drill down later but for the moment all you need to do is jot down what immediately comes to mind. A word of caution—some people sit and think, and others just sit.

Welcome back. I will assume you have been able to answer all the questions [other than point 3 if you are unemployed] and are ready to analyze your answers.

The purpose of this exercise is to get you to THINK about what it is you have in mind and whether at first glance it is feasible. What you also have is the beginnings of your BUSINESS PLAN.

It is important to take your time with this exercise. I encourage my first-time clients to do the exercise on their own and then, if they choose, to do it again with their spouse or partner and maybe even with a trusted friend or a mentor. There are 2 reasons for suggesting a second visit. It provides an alternative perspective on your thinking as well as ensuring that it involves your spouse or partner in the whole process from the very beginning [a point I will keep banging away at].

Now would be a good time to get into the habit of doing research. If you have ever bought a property [or similar large asset] you will understand the necessity of doing your homework [in the form of research] and doing it thoroughly. This logic applies even more so when starting a business. There are no short cuts or benefits in getting someone else to do the research for you. This business is your future, so you need to get your hands dirty from day one. Bad research and planning or the lack thereof will cause bad implementation during start-up so don't mess with this aspect of your future business. Do this step properly and avoid an enormous amount of regret and disillusionment later.

Time to examine and evaluate each question and your answers. The important one first.

1. What business am I going to start?

Making this decision can be both fun and seriously frustrating.

Owning your own business is not a job, it is a lifetime commitment and must be something you look forward to doing each day, and even on weekends. Passion is great, but you also need to know what you are doing. Being passionate about making and selling cupcakes is maybe something you can relate to, but if you cannot boil water successfully, you may need to be looking at an alternative business idea.

If you are one of the fortunate folks who knows what it is you want to do, then move onto the second question [**Can I do it from home?**], if not, read on.

My experience has shown that these lists go from one extreme to the other. Very short or excessively long. Some folks will fall back on their more recent employment–the last or current job, and nothing wrong with that.

Some other options include hobbies, part-time interests or other activities you have always enjoyed doing will also spring to mind. I have to admit though, that after many years of doing the same job [and being reasonably good at it but intensely bored] the last thing I wanted to do was start a business which would be a continuation of what I had been doing in the past. Which, as you would have already read, is exactly what I ended up doing.

Hopefully, it is different for you.

If your first instinct is to fall back on what you have been doing during your working career, but not sure how to convert it into a business offering, here are some points to ponder.

- Consider what you have been doing throughout your working career and not just your last position, list all those other activities or functions you got involved with. Maybe you also managed the company soccer team or became the first choice in finding charities to sponsor.

- What are you qualified to do–do you have a degree in engineering for example? I know entrepreneurs who, although academically qualified in a particular field, have in fact, never pursued a corporate career in that field. Maybe time to consider digging out that qualification scroll and giving it some thought?

- Which element/s of your career was/were the most successful?

- Were you exposed to other aspects or functions that you found intriguing or interesting at the time but could not pursue? For example, as an engineer on a project you were exposed to Project Management but at the time could not further your interest.

- If you work in the corporate environment and your company practices the sport of annual performance assessments, look back on these, they should give you an idea of what your management saw as your strengths and weaknesses.

If nothing bites you immediately or you have no interest in pursuing your past profession, there are other resources to check out.

- Ask one or two close family members, friends or colleagues that you know will be open and honest with you [avoid folks who will tell you want they think you want to hear], what they think you are passionate about, or better still, good at. You could well be pleasantly surprised at the outcome.

- There are many articles on the web about home business opportunities and it is worth having a look through them.

Here are several articles from Entrepreneur.com listing numerous professions suitable for home or small business

10 Types of Businesses You Can Build After 5 p.m.

20 Business Ideas for Stay-at-Home Parents

55 Surefire Home-based Businesses You Can Start for Under $5,000

63 Businesses to Start for Under $10,000

Just a thought about online-based businesses which I know are often new entrepreneurs first choice and for many good reasons.

Starting an online business offers many enticements to an aspirant home business owner. Products are easy to come by and the start-up costs are minimal as is the training.

However, I am at pains to point out that most of the struggling business owners who approach me for help have launched online enterprises, and what appears to be a common problem is the lack of research and planning. They know someone who has started a similar business, or they have read articles on how to make "a $1000 a day online" and assume that launching an online business is easy pickings.

Wrong! It is probably one of the most competitive industries to enter and requires even more planning than your average brick and mortar business. Allow me to quote an example. Recently a friend asked me to help his son whose online business had crashed within 3 months of start-up. The products being offered were in the high-end technical market and when I inquired as to the prospective customer base all I got was a blank look and the response "well, everyone on the Internet in South Africa". In my country, only 54% of the population of 58 million have access to the Internet [compared to say New Zealand with a population of just over 4 million and a usage statistic of almost 90%] and only a relatively small portion of that limited customer base would have the technical knowledge and user skills to be attracted to this product range never mind being able to afford it!

So, although very attractive at first glance the world of online business can be difficult.

With that said, if you are still at a loss or confused about what it is you would like to do here is an exercise that may help expand your thinking towards business opportunities.

This can be done in a spreadsheet if you are familiar with the software or if not, time to grab more blank pages [you may want to open a file or folder to keep all these pages in for later reference].

What am I passionate about?

Here you want to list those things that get the blood flowing and get you excited [no not that!]. For example, writing stories or articles, experimenting with new food recipes, painting, lecturing or training others, home or car repairs, and so on. Let the creative and imaginative juices flow. By the way, watching TV and playing video games do not qualify, although I have to be cautious here, there are Youtubers and full-time gamers who make more than a reasonable return on their efforts.

Rate your list with your greatest passion at the top, followed sequentially by the others.

What am I good at?

This is different to what you are passionate about, and sometimes, you may hate doing them, for example, you may be accomplished at doing repair jobs around the house but hate it with a passion. List them anyway. Some other examples are repairing computers, doing oil and lube changes on your car, cooking, interacting with children, etc.

Think about current and past jobs. Not just the main responsibilities but other aspects. For example, if your career path has been in IT Management but you have also enjoyed, and are good at, repairing computers, then that is what you would list.

The trick here is to avoid becoming emotional about your list—don't try to decide whether you like, or otherwise, what the idea represents. Just write it down.

Rate your list, with the activity you are best at on the top.

What do I really want to do?

This may appear to be covered by your passions; however, the idea here is to get you to think bigger picture. For example, you may have always wanted your own restaurant. If your passion is cooking and you are comfortable with people, then you have just defined your long-term business goal.

Don't worry if nothing jumps up and slaps you in the face at this early stage.

What do I hate doing?

This step establishes if there are any counterbalances to the first 3 options. This list should also include what you know you are not any good at. You may be passionate about antique furniture, but if you are no good at basic woodwork, restoring old furniture is not an option in the short term.

Let's use the restaurant example above. A dislike of cooking or an inability to deal with people could mean you should be looking at alternative business opportunities.

Regarding your current job, which aspects do you dislike, or you suck at and why? Think about your weaknesses; for example, if working with numbers is a problem you need to list it.

Got your lists? Good. You may want to try to score the various points but my opinion is that as you drew up the list, the chances of you being unbiased in your scoring is unlikely—no worry it's only human.

The next step is to look through your lists and identify two or more potential opportunities for a new business. Draw from options 1 through 3 and then highlight any potential obstacles from option 4. Take your time.

Rate your short list. Don't try to analyze your choices at this stage. Put the one that excites you the most at the top and follow with the others.

So which type of business is the best option?

It is now time to review your short list of business ideas to determine which one is the most suitable. If there is more than one idea on your list, you will need to ask the following questions for each idea. Your outcome is to identify which idea grabs you the most as a possible business venture.

Question: Is my idea saleable?

You may be passionate about watching paint dry and be very good at it, but you will have serious problems trying to convince someone to pay you to do it.

To help answer this question, you will need to establish whether others are already in the market or if there is a demand that is not being met. A quick look through local newspapers, telephone directories, Yellow Pages, and all that junk mail you get will provide an answer. A yes or no is all you are looking for at this stage.

Competition shouldn't put you off. Although you do not want to go head to head with a Microsoft, remember that competition is not a bad thing. It means Joe Public is buying what you are hoping to sell.

However, be realistic. If you intend to offer after-school Child Care and your initial research shows that there are 10 Child Care Centers in your area, you either live in a very large suburb or your intended market is saturated.

Question: Do I have the necessary skill set to provide the service or produce the product? Will I need further training?

This is where "my passions" and "what I do well" may be out of sync.

Let me use an example. One of your ideas is to locate antique furniture, restore it and sell the finished piece, something you have always been passionate about. Your woodwork skills are passable, but it may not be enough to convince your buyers that your restoration work has added value to the piece of furniture.

Do you undergo woodwork training–and for how long and at what cost? Or do you employ additional skilled resources?

Question: Can I do all the work on my own to start with?

If the answer to the question for the antique furniture about needing additional skilled resources was YES, will you have enough funding at start-up to pay a skilled artisan? You must highlight this requirement to include in your funding equation for the Financial Plan [Part 2].

Question: Do I require any specialized equipment for the business?

Here I am referring to equipment that would be used directly in the manufacturing process that you do not already own. For example, you may need a lathe to restore the antique furniture or a very large cooker to prepare your curries in. If you intend selling cupcakes to all the coffee shops in your area, will the family sedan be adequate for the deliveries?

Do you already have a computer and printer with Internet connectivity? Is there any other office equipment you may need, such as installing a land line?

Extra equipment means extra start-up funding.

Question: Is there adequate space in the house/garage/flat that will allow me to do the business?

Using the antique furniture example again, if you cannot convert your garage into a suitable workshop, you may have a work area problem. You don't want to be using your family room or lounge area as a carpenter shop, the family may find it intrusive, to put it mildly.

If you haven't already been talking to your partner [or family] about your idea now is most definitely the time.

Ideally, you need to have an office from which to work from. If you already have a study or cubbyhole where you have been able to shut yourself off from the rest of the house, this is your new *company headquarters*. If not, you need to find a compromise that affords you a "secluded work station" but does not create an intolerable inconvenience for the other members of the household.

2. Can I legally do it from home?

Location, location, location!

Duh! I thought this is a home-based business? Well, yes, assuming that what you have in mind does not disrupt the neighborhood. If you intend to manufacture wrought-iron gates in your garage all the cutting, welding and grinding are more than likely to attract the attention of your entire neighborhood and I guarantee you will be the subject of numerous complaints to your local municipality.

Check with the local authorities as to what is allowable and what is not. Having dozens of clients parked outside your house may be permissible but will be annoying to your neighbors.

Let your neighbors know what you intend to do and get them on board. In some countries, the municipal By-Laws requires that you get the written permission of your neighbors to start a home-based business. Check with your local authority.

Above all, be considerate to those in your street.

3. Can I tell my boss to take a hike or should I wait?

When I first started out on my own, one of my emotional drivers was imagining the day, I could tell my boss where to shove his job. To be honest, when the time or should I say times, came around I found that I didn't have the pent-up anger I had imagined, and so the parting of ways was amicable–just goes to show.

Don't forget, you might want to pitch to your ex-employer for work in the future, so assess your emotions with a touch of logic.

This question is part of the whole financing issue. If you are supporting a family do you have enough financial reserves to allow you to resign your job and continue surviving and funding the new business on what you have in the piggy bank?

If not, stay where you are and build up the reserve. Get the family, or those dependent on you, on board and everyone working towards the same goal.

4. What impact will my idea have on my family, friends, or loved ones?

This is very much a personal issue and you are the only one who can assess what you need, but it is important that you give it the necessary attention.

Some thoughts on the subject.

If you are the major breadwinner in the family, your partner will also share the risk and will experience the stress and worry over the viability of your decision to go it alone. This is of special relevance if you are the sole income source for the family.

Once you have decided on where to locate your office, this area, which was once part of the family domain, will become a "no go area", no doubt causing disruption, especially for the little ones.

The general routine of the household will be disrupted—you will be at home as opposed to being away for a good 8-10 hours a day during the week and you probably will work in your "no go area" on weekends, instead of being asleep most of the time [joke].

Both you and your partner will be stressed out, tired and likely to be short on patience during the early months of the business—which may be difficult for the kids to understand and appreciate.

There are also some rules that the family needs to understand. One of the biggest difficulties that new home-based business owners encounter in the first months of operation, which incidentally has nothing to do with business, is the apparent assumption by other members of the family, that since you are at home, you should be able to do all those other things that need doing. For example, being the household driver, milk and bread buyer, and the "just please do this and just please do that" call upon service.

Avoid this if at all possible. It does not mean that you get excused from contributing to the household activities as normal, but the family needs to be prepared to cut you some slack, especially in the beginning. Your workday has not changed; the only difference is your usual 8 hours of work are being done at home and not at some distant office location.

I won't labor the point any further other than to reiterate—talk to those close to you. Make it a team event. It can make the difference between short-term failure and long-term success.

Making your choice

All that is left to do now is decide as to the nature of your proposed business. There is not a lot of advice that can be offered at this stage other than if split between two possibilities, following your gut instinct is not a bad way to go.

However, should you feel that you cannot commit 100% to one or more of your ideas, there is nothing wrong in putting your decision on the back burner for the moment.

We will construct the various elements of your plan through Part 2. Completing the whole process could also provide greater insight into which possibility to pursue and so wait until these steps are complete before making a final decision.

Please note: this will mean that if you have more than one possibility, you will need to complete each element of the plan for each of your choices.

HAVING A BUSINESS PARTNER

Other then the traditional "mom and pop" business I have not encountered many home-based business start-ups that were founded on a partnership although there is no plausible reason why they can't work.

Why would you need a partner? There are several reasons some of which could include the need for a financial provider, a great idea developed by two people together, extra hands to cope with the anticipated workload or just two folks who really will enjoy working together.

For me the only criteria that needs to be addressed, right at the outset, is that the partnership arrangement is formalized. It must clearly state the ownership share and the responsibilities and accountabilities of each partner with special emphasis on how decisions are made. The manner in which profits and losses are shared must be spelled out and what the plan is in the eventuality that one partner may wish to leave the business.

Forming your Company

Now that you have decided on the type of company you want, it is time to register your company and create a legal entity through which you will trade. One of the first questions for the company registration process is: what is your company name?

The rule of thumb when deciding on the name is that it should reflect what the business is about: Joe's Plumbing Service, Big Time Web Design, are examples. This rule belies the fact that many of the biggest brands around the world are single names, but I'm sure you get the idea. If the company name provides guidance about what is on offer, it makes it easier for customers to find you. This process is similar to finding a usable domain name for a website.

You will need to think of at least 5 possible names and the reason for this is that when you apply to register your company, you may find your first preferences are already taken. A quick way to check is to type the proposed name/s into Google and see what comes up. In some countries, the Company Registrar will accept a new company name if the full name, or initials and surname, of the owner, are included in the company name, even though there may be a clash with existing companies. You may have to add something to your name such as "consulting" or "home repairs".

Once you decide on the name for your company, get it registered as soon as possible. Each country has its own laws for company registration, and you should be able to find out what they are on government web sites or through a friendly local accountant. Some processes take days and others can be months, but you will get the name reserved even though the formal process of registering the company may take some time.

You will probably be able to complete the registration yourself; however, there are consultants who will, for a fee I would imagine, do it on your behalf.

ALL THAT LEGAL STUFF

Being the owner of a legal entity necessitates an understanding of what, legally, your obligations will be. Again, each country has its own laws and the onus will be on you to establish exactly what it requires of you and the future company. I have found that often a small statutory requirement overlooked in the beginning can derail your whole campaign just as you are about to get launched.

HINT: Do it correctly, don't get torpedoed by bureaucracy at the last minute.

Expert Advice

Either before start-up or during the first year of operation, it is possible that you may require external help to assist with a specific problem.

Here are some possibilities.

Accountant: If you don't do well with figures and find no pleasure in getting two columns of numbers to balance then look for an accountant, preferably someone who is <u>not</u> a friend or relative.

If you feel comfortable managing your own financials, there are some very good accounting software packages for small and home businesses that often include training. In Part 2, I explain how I used Excel spreadsheets to create my financial, marketing and sales budgets, which is one alternative to purchasing an accounting package.

Check what General Accounting Policies and Practices apply in your country for the company. For example, you may require an external auditing company to compile your year-end financial returns for company tax purposes.

Lawyer: Some experts on business start-ups will tell you it is essential to have a lawyer from the start. I don't know what lawyers charge per hour in your country, but in my country; it is exorbitant. Unless you have identified a legal issue up front [a problem with municipal by-laws or a need to lodge a Patent application are examples] hire one only when you need to.

Tax Consultant: These folks are helpful with understanding what your tax obligations will be, be it personal, company or sales related. They can also assist with identifying the best company type for your intended business.

Statutory Requirements

What statutory requirements apply in setting up a new company in your country? The legal requirements for setting up a company are well documented and explained by the relevant authorities in all the countries I have operated in and there are government and Association web sites which offer detailed information.

Many governments sites have brochures or books that you can download and are a great help in assisting with the legal stuff.

Usual Legal Requirements

Company name reservation

Company registration

Company tax registration and submission of returns [when, how, etc.]

Company documentation and formation requirements. This could include a list of directors, Notice of Incorporation and Memorandum of Association. It will depend on the type of company you are registering.

Sales or Value-Added taxes—if applicable

Format and frequency of submission of the company financial statements

Storage of company financial and other records [how long, where, etc.]

Any specific requirements related to employees [unemployment insurance, medical support, etc.—which is only applicable if you will employ staff]

COMPANY STRUCTURE

This refers to the type of company that you can establish and again this will depend on what the accepted practice is in your country.

In my country, for example, the following PROFIT generating companies are permissible and preferred by home and small business owners:

1. Sole Proprietor.

Also known as a sole trader. It is a structure that allows you to trade as yourself. Your company name would be something like Joe Blogs trading as Joe Blogs Repairs if you repair vehicles. This is the simplest form of company configuration and requires virtually no effort to set up and get going. You need to inform the taxman of your extra income. The biggest risk for this structure is that if the business fails, your creditors can take all your assets: your house, your car, your furniture–anything to recover the money you owe them because you are the business. There is no separation between your personal assets and liabilities and those of the business. You cannot have partners as a sole proprietor, only employees.

2. *Private Company.*

Also known as a Proprietary Limited or Pty Ltd company. This is the most popular structure for entrepreneurs who want to have the advantages of running their business as a company. Essentially, a new entity [think of it as an imaginary or juristic "person"] is created. This legal entity is separate from you as are the profits and losses. It will have the owners [shareholders] which may be one or more persons who own the company and the managers [directors] who run the company. Sometimes these are the same people, but not necessarily.

3. *Partnerships*

A partnership exists between two or more persons.

Each person contributes money, property or skills and expects to share in the profits or losses of the partnership. A partnership must file annual information returns but does not pay company income tax. All income tax is paid by the individuals in their own capacity, professional folks such as doctors and lawyers are some examples of partnerships.

Again, the information sites about forming a company will explain the options available in your country, or better still consult an Accounting or Tax Consulting company for guidance.

HINT: It may also be helpful to talk to people who have been through the process. Someone you know who already operates a successful business who can discuss all the options, benefits, and obligations with you in person.

Home Business Benefits: You must inquire from your government authorities if there are any benefits accruable to a Home Business owner. For example, in South Africa, certain categories of small business types have a company annual income tax threshold below which they pay no company tax. This is based on the company's annual earnings; if below a certain figure, the company is exempt.

You also receive a rebate on your personal income tax in the form of a portion of your home expenses, such as mortgage payments and utility charges which are attributable to the running of the business.

Other legal considerations

Value Added or Sales Tax

As with company tax and if applicable, you need to know the rules in terms of how these taxes will affect your sales price and how to submit the proceeds to the Revenue authorities. A word of caution here: if you intend to sell internationally, please ensure that you discuss sales tax provisions applicable in the countries to which you intend to offer your products with an expert. You must understand the tax laws governing sales of goods or services to other countries. The EU is a case in point. The requirements can be tricky and many a website owner offering digital goods has found themselves on the wrong side of the taxman by not acquainting themselves with the fine print of the relevant Acts.

Insurance

If you have a private insurance broker contact him or her [if not look for insurance companies that specialize in working with new small businesses] and establish what additional insurance is needed to cover you as the business owner [sometimes called a Key Person Insurance], your office equipment, assets [e.g. company vehicle if you purchase one] and staff if you intend to employ.

An insurance that is worth having, if you don't already have one in your private capacity, is what is sometimes referred to as Public Liability or Third-Party insurance. This covers injury or death to third parties on your premises, such as visiting clients, suppliers, delivery personnel or other folks related to the business.

Intellectual Property, Trademarks, Copyright & Patents

If you intend to be a writer, poet, blogger, artist, inventor or you think you have a great idea for a unique product then you need to put some thought to protecting your rights in your work. But first, this description covers an explanation of what Intellectual Property means.

Intellectual property [IP] is a term referring to creations of the intellect for which a monopoly is assigned to designated owners by law. Some common types of intellectual property rights [IPR] are trademarks, copyright, patents, industrial design rights, and in some jurisdictions trade secrets: all these cover music, literature, and other artistic works; discoveries and inventions; and words, phrases, symbols, and designs. [source: Wikipedia]

In practice, originators protect their work with one or more of the following elements of IP.

Trademark

Entrepreneur.com, in its *Small Business Encyclopedia* section, defines and explains a Trademark as:

"Definition: Any symbol, word or combination thereof used to represent or identify a product. A service mark means the same thing but identifies a service.

Trademarks and service marks are applied to a manufacturer's or a seller's products and services to distinguish them in the marketplace - a valuable marketing tool, in some circumstances. A trademark or service mark prevents another person from offering a similar product or service confusingly similar to yours. If you don't register your trademark, you may be prohibited from using it by someone who has."

The following symbols may designate a trademark:

TM   [the "trademark symbol", which is the letters "TM", for an unregistered trademark, a mark used to promote or brand goods]

SM   [which is the letters "SM" in superscript, for an unregistered service mark, a mark used to promote or brand services]

®   [the letter "R" surrounded by a circle, for a registered trademark]

Examples of Trademarks

There are many examples of trademarks all around us and we make use of trademarked products daily. ***Bitlaw.com*** lists the following everyday examples of where trademarks have been used:

Letters and words	- Apple, IBM, Netscape, Silicon Graphics
Logos style design	- McDonald's double arches, NBC's peacock
Pictures or drawings MSN's butterfly	- Apple's Automator, Corning's Pink Panther,

Combination

[letters & a design]   - Java Powered, Silicon Graphics, Sun

Slogans	- "Just do it", "I'm loving it"
Product shape	- Coke bottle, Apple's iPod
Sounds	- NBC's three-tone chime

It is worth reading Bitlaw"s article on *Trademarks and the Internet* as it speaks to the use of, and infringements of, trademarks on web sites and their relation to domain names.

I also came across, courtesy of the web site of Attorneys at Law – **Widerman & Malek**, some other interesting examples of trademarks:

Catchphrases TV reality show	- "You're Fired", used by Donald Trump in a
Figure or mascot	- Geico's talking gecko.

Lyrics   - A songwriter's lyrics are trademarks. According to Wilderman & Malek *"A songwriter"s lyrics are trademarks. Bob Seger and the Silver Bullet Band made a hit single song "Like a Rock" in 1986. In 1991, this song helped Chevrolet bounce back from a near bankruptcy situation. The "Like a Rock" commercials were so successful that these commercials were used for over ten years. Chevrolet paid Seger royalties for licensing his trademark, "Like a Rock"."*

To get a Trademark you will have to register it with the relevant authority in your country. The sooner the better.

Copyright

This is an important aspect of Intellectual Property rights that you should know if you intend to own a web site or publish articles, write books, blogs or display images owned by others.

Wikipedia explains copyright:

"Copyright is a legal right created by the law of a country that grants the creator of an original work exclusive rights for its use and distribution. This is usually only for a limited time. The exclusive rights are not absolute but limited by limitations and exceptions to copyright law, including fair use."

Its practical uses are laid out in an article at **Plagiarism Today** titled *What is Copyright* and I have reproduced the first 2 paragraphs by way of explanation:

"Fundamentally, copyright is a law that gives you ownership over the things you create. Be it a painting, a photograph, a poem or a novel, if you created it, you own it and it's the copyright law itself that assures that ownership. The ownership that copyright law grants comes with several rights that you, as the owner, have exclusively. Those rights include:

The right to reproduce the work

to prepare derivative works

to distribute copies

to perform the work

and to display the work publicly

These are your rights and your rights alone. Unless you willingly give them up [EX: A Creative Commons License], no one can violate them legally. This means that, unless you say otherwise, no one can perform a piece written by you or make copies of it, even with attribution, unless you give the OK."

I recommend that you take the time to read the whole article as it highlights the copyright infringements that many writers, bloggers, photographers, and other artistic entrepreneurs encounter on the Internet. Please don't undermine the hard work and talents of others by ignoring their intellectual property rights.

If you have ever used image sites such as Flickr you will have encountered A Creative Commons License. You may also have seen this at the bottom of a web site you follow – © 2009-2015 Joe Blogs. This means that it protects the content of that site for the period stated.

It is important to note that unlike other forms of intellectual property rights, such as patents, trademark and design rights which arise only after registration with the relevant authority in your country, registration for the copyright to exist is unnecessary. If you are the originator of a piece of work, you have copyright ownership.

Patents

Registering a patent is an expensive and complex undertaking and before you consider protecting your work with a patent discuss the process with your local Patent Attorneys. Owning and protecting a patent requires almost full-time knowledge of what others in your industry are doing in terms of inventions, designs, and manufacturing. To protect one of my patents required a full-time attorney who did nothing other than check for applications by others, daily, that may have been infringing my patent and which then allowed us to lodge objections to those applications in time to block them. A very expensive exercise. As with Trademarks and Copyrights, each country has its own Patent Laws.

The United States Patent and Trademark Office explains a patent for the USA:

"A patent for an invention is the grant of a property right to the inventor, issued by the United States Patent and Trademark Office. Generally, the term of a new patent is 20 years from the

date on which the application for the patent was filed in the United States or, in special cases, from the date an earlier related application was filed, subject to the payment of maintenance fees. U.S. patent grants are effective only within the United States, U.S. territories, and U.S. possessions. Under certain circumstances, patent term extensions or adjustments may be available.

The right conferred by the patent grant is, in the language of the statute and of the grant itself, "the right to exclude others from making, using, offering for sale, or selling" the invention in the United States or "importing" the invention into the United States. What is granted is not the right to make, use, offer for sale, sell or import, but the right to exclude others from making, using, offering for sale, selling or importing the invention. Once a patent is issued, the patentee must enforce the patent without aid of the USPTO."

There are three types of patents:

1] Utility patents may be granted to anyone who invents or discovers any new and useful process, machine, article of manufacture, or composition of matter, or any new and useful improvement thereof;

2] Design patents may be granted to anyone who invents an original, and ornamental design for an article of manufacture; and

3] Plant patents may be granted to anyone who invents or discovers and asexually reproduces any distinct and new variety of plant.

The Patent laws in each country will be different so please ensure you talk to the right authorities BEFORE you consider getting a patent.

To summarize

Let's look back at what we have covered.

In the second element of Part 1 we looked at the administrative processes that are necessary to get your idea converted into a legal trading entity.

Specifically, we explored the procedural side of setting up a small business.

- Deciding on the type of business you will have.
- The legal requirements associated with the formation of a company.
- And an overview of the complex world of patents, trademarks, and patents

As I mentioned in the opening of Part 1, it has all been about YOU as a potential home business owner. The purpose is to prepare you for the exciting journey ahead as you begin turning your dream into a reality. I hope that I have been able to demystify some aspects of ownership while providing you with the assurance that you too can do it.

There is no reason you cannot succeed–you just need to get your head into the right space, manage your fears and inhibitions.

From home cooking to innovative inventions, people all around the world are turning to self-employment and many will continue to do so in the future.

The home-based entrepreneur is now accepted as a substantial contributor to any country's GDP and governments and large private sector companies are acknowledging that home-based businesses can be a significant launch pad towards economic growth and job creation.

The desire to be "your own boss" comes from more than just your current annoyance and frustration with your employment circumstance. Although having total control over our destiny is unlikely for most of us, but being able to influence the extent and quality of your daily output, is without parallel.

The ability to influence the subsequent amount of return for your effort, and achieve your personal goals and aspirations will make all the effort and sacrifices worth it.

See you in Part 2!

PART 2 - The first 6 Steps in the process

Introduction

*Planning is bringing the future into the present
so that you can do something about it now.
Alan Lakein*

The Day BEFORE the Day AFTER

You have only a few items left to pack and then, FREEDOM!

The copy of your University Degree, all the certificates and awards from your years in the corporate world, your favorite pen, the slow swinging metallic balls that drove your boss mad and the wall clock they gave you after ten years of dedicated service to the corporate master, are all stowed away in a cardboard box.

It's time to leave the office for one last time.

No, you have not been laid off; you are leaving to start your own home-based business.

For the last month, you have been bragging to your mates about all the money you will make, the free time you will have to do all those things on your bucket list, the exotic vacations you will take and let's not forget upgrading the car and getting that seriously large TV screen.

You have said your farewells to those, soon to be ex-colleagues, and spent 10 glorious minutes with the boss articulating where, on his anatomy, he can shove the job.

Sure, there were some good times at the company, but you always knew you were made for greater things and now the time has arrived to fulfill your dreams. As you leave the company building, you force yourself to ignore the impulse to look back over your shoulder for one last time.

You also suppress that nagging sensation in the pit of your stomach, which you have been feeding with large amounts of antacid medication for the last 2 weeks, that there is something that just does not feel right.

You are ready for new and greater things. The first day of your new life as a home-based business owner has just begun.

The Day AFTER the Day BEFORE

You're awake but it wasn't the alarm clock that woke you. "Damn! Late again for work," is your immediate reaction. Hey, hold up there a minute. You realize you don't have a job. You're unemployed. "Oh ?%&, what have I done?"

After the initial panic abates you lie back, smile and take a deep breath. The first day of your new life has just dawned.

You, like millions of others before you, have taken the giant leap of faith and started your own HOME-BASED BUSINESS.

After months and months of researching and planning for the big day, it has arrived, and you are ready for launch.

Sorry, what was that?

What research and what plan you say.

You don't have a plan for your new business?

Nobody told you that you would need one?

Really, did you ask someone who has a business or knows something about starting a new business whether you would need one?

No?

Oh dear, I think there is a real probability your new business will fail. Maybe you should have paid more attention to that nagging feeling.

> *"If you fail to plan, you are planning to fail!"*
>
> *— Benjamin Franklin*

Being a home business owner can be a lonely profession.

As the business owner, it is incumbent upon you and you alone to make the telling decisions; besides having to multi-task most of the time. After all my successes, failures, and roles as both mentee and mentor, it is obvious that to improve your chances of ultimate success; you must have a PLAN.

How detailed a plan is contingent upon the complexity of the undertaking, but if a sustainable business is your goal a realistic and implementable plan as to how you intend to ensure that sustainability is imperative.

To have a workable plan you will need to do the research, and research, if done correctly, takes time and patience. You will need to get comfortable with approaching other people, asking questions, tapping into their knowledge base on a given subject and learning how to be a good listener.

As with any plan, there must be a start and end point.

I am not suggesting you re-invent the wheel but what I am suggesting is that you accept that you are the catalyst that will make your business succeed and so the more you can learn, and therefore implement in your entrepreneurial journey, the more self-sufficient and reliable you will become. Your decisions will be less prone to risk and your self-belief when you make them will lead to success.

It is your business so take ownership in everything related to it, from day one. Part of this ownership is understanding your limits and so deciding to seek external help is not a sign of weakness or incompetence. It is a sign of business maturity and is one of the essential foundation hallmarks of a successful entrepreneur.

So, let's get planning.

To quote Walt Disney:

> *"The way to get started is to quit talking and begin doing."*

As with any plan; document the processes you apply and the progress you make. This will help you readjust your plan as your business grows. Get into the habit of continuously reviewing your initial idea and subsequent adjustments to make sure you remain on track.

You need to design a filing system, digital or hard copy, to keep track of everything you record.

A system I found useful was to use a whiteboard or large piece of cardboard. As I developed my ideas and expanded them into processes and milestones, I recorded each element on post-its and pasted them in the appropriate blocks on my board. Once the initial plan was designed, I transcribed into a digital version which became the foundation of my filing system.

I have since migrated to Mind Mapping software.

Although in this Part 2 I will share ideas and suggested activities on how to research and define the various elements of your business plan, please accept that they are suggestions only and not the only and finite way to complete a task. Please feel free to expand on them and look for other innovative ways to accomplish each step. This is your dream, you can write the dialogue any which way that best suits you.

And remember—have some fun as well!

Planning your Business

Let our advance worrying become advance thinking and planning.
Winston Churchill

I am sure that during your school, college, or working career you have come across the term BUSINESS PLAN. The **have to have** for all business owners. In my opinion, there are 2 forms of a business plan, the first is what I refer to as the "formal" document, and the second is what I call the PLAN FOR YOUR BUSINESS, which is less formal in its presentation but equally important.

So, what is a Business Plan as opposed to a Plan for my Business?

Entrepreneur.com's SMALL BUSINESS ENCYCLOPEDIA defines and explains the formal Business Plan:

"Definition: A written document describing the nature of the business, the sales and marketing strategy, and the financial background, and containing a projected profit-and-loss statement.

A business plan is also a road map that provides directions so a business can plan its future and helps it avoid bumps in the road. The time you spend making your business plan thorough and accurate and keeping it up-to-date is an investment that pays big dividends in the long term.

Your business plan should conform to accepted guidelines regarding form and content. Each section should include specific elements and address relevant questions that the people who read your plan will most likely ask."

The above document also contains a list and description of each of the components generally found in a Business Plan

Do you need a formal Business Plan?

If you intend to approach a third party for help, be it an individual or an organization, you need a formal Business Plan. It could be an application for funding, a proposal for a joint venture or approaching a potential business partner.

In support of this recommendation, I urge you to use a professional to compile the document on your behalf; preferably a professional with a financial background and someone you can meet with on a face-to-face basis as and when needed. You will only get one crack at impressing your potential partner or investor with your idea, so spend the time and money on getting the very best Plan developed—it will be worth it.

However, please note that whether you choose to use a professional to compile your plan or elect to draw it up yourself, the information needed in both cases is the same. The professional will have no idea what your business is about, so you need to fill in the blanks.

Do you need a Plan for your Business?

Absolutely, irrespective of whether you do a formal Plan or informally document the most important elements of how your business will operate, YOU NEED A PLAN.

And it is this informal Plan for your Business that we will construct in this Book.

In simplistic terms, the plan for your business is your intent and understanding of the business you will launch, what you intend to offer and what you hope to achieve with it and, if you meet all expectations, where you hope to go with it.

It is important that you compile your plan in a structured way to be confident you have incorporated all the important aspects. If you browsed through the formal Business Plan examples in the above article, you would have noticed that it follows a systematic layout in presenting the facts about the intended business, its goals, and proposed outcomes.

Some information required is necessary when applying for a loan, for example, a bank will require to know where the business is located, and your personal details, etc., but is not required for our purposes. We will however use this tried and tested template to formulate your idea and concept and turn them into the Plan for your Business.

The business plan is a **work in progress** so do not file it away in some dark hole after completing it: it is a working, living and dynamic document which will provide the engine room for your business. The document must be updated and ready to hand at all times, as and when your circumstances require it. As your day-to-day operations, needs, and financial situation changes so you will need to re-evaluate your goals and targets in the plan. Most small businesses fail within the first 18 months of a start-up, so if you going to beat that statistic, you need to have a solid plan.

The Plan for your Business

For those who do not need a formal Business Plan and have opted rather for the more informal Plan for the Business, I will cover the main points that your plan needs to incorporate. It is important that you understand that the idea here is to create a WRITTEN document and not just a list of bullet points. Having a backed up, typed version stored on your computer hard drive is the way to go. This will allow you to update it as and when necessary.

Your Plan will essentially consist of 6 components or STEPS:

1. Defining the business—what you do and what you have to sell.

2. The Product—what it is, what it will cost and the proposed selling price.

3. A Marketing Plan—where you intend to sell your product, what it will look like, how to sell it, and profiling your intended customers.

4. Growth Plan—the vision for the future including a Resource Plan—people you may employ.

5. A Financial Plan—funding, budgets, and payment terms.

6. Business analysis—the strengths, weaknesses, opportunities, and threats.

Let's get started with the first component.

Step 1 - Defining the business

> *Adventure is just bad planning.*
> Roald Amundsen

We spent a great deal of time in Part 1 discussing the various business options and alternatives. I have to assume that you are clear in your mind what the business will be about and what products or services it will offer. What you now need to do is "define" in precise detail what your company is all about. It will also help you create a brand around your product.

This definition will take 2 forms—a more detailed description, about 10 lines long that will explain:

- what the business is about;
- what products or services it will offer;
- what in the way of value add it will provide to customers and why will it be different, and
- the intended market it will access.

The reason for this step is not only to clarify in your own mind what it is you will do but the definition or company mission statement is something that an outsider needs to understand. If a total stranger should happen upon your description, he or she must understand at first glance what your business is all about.

You might start by asking, and answering, the questions a third party would ask when first encountering your company. For example.

Q. What is the product?

A. For the purpose of this exercise, let's assume it is cupcakes.

Q. What are you going to do with your cupcakes?

A. Sell them to the public.

Q. How and where?

A. Through local home industry outlets and bakeries, which are in my local community.

Q. Why should people buy your cupcakes?

A. We will offer unique flavors and wherever possible use health-conscious ingredients.

This is very simplistic, but it should give you an idea about what you are trying to share.

Here is an example of a brief introduction for the product of a technology company I part owned some years ago and which had designed, developed and manufactured a PC security product.

"[Name of company] an RFID technology design and development company, provides a unique computer security product [name of the product if it has one] that will enable a user to not only prevent unauthorized access, but more importantly, it will secure the valuable, and at times irreplaceable, data stored on the computer.

No smart cards, password or biometrics required, just walk away from your computer and it will LOCK. When you return, it will unlock at precisely the screen you were using when you locked it.

It is compliant with [international certifications listed here] and uses leading-edge RFID technology and environmentally friendly components. After a lengthy period of field trials, the product is now available for all computer users, irrespective of make or Operating System".

This presentation highlights the following issues:

- it tells you who the company is and what it does for a living;
- explains what the product on offer is - a PC security product and briefly describes what it does;
- its primary function is to protect the PC when it is unattended, unauthorized users cannot gain access to send emails, etc., in your name;
- the "value add" is that if the PC is lost or stolen, the baddie cannot gain access to the valuable data on the hard drive;
- it highlights that it differs from other similar security products already in the market;
- the product complies with all the international technical and safety regulations;
- includes all the latest technology, and
- is applicable to any PC and has been field tested before being released into the market and so is "bug-free".

What was consciously left out was a more detailed explanation of how it worked. This omission was very successful in prompting the first question from a potential customer, "so how does it work". That left the door open for the salesperson to climb in boots and all and get agreement for a live demonstration. It almost always worked. In this case, we also used the description in marketing presentations and advertising pamphlets and slots.

Besides the lengthier definition of your business, you also need to come up with an extended **one-liner** or sales pitch, often referred to these days as an "elevator pitch". It should take you about 20 to 30 seconds [the average length of time for an elevator ride, hence the name] to describe what you do.

Using the PC product example, the elevator pitch went something like this:

"We manufacture an RFID product that will allow you to secure your PC by locking and unlocking it without you even having to touch the machine. No passwords, smart cards or biometrics needed. It will stop unauthorized access and protect your valuable data."

The usual response was:

"What, seriously, no cards, passwords or fingerprints? Explain more, I'm interested."

The idea with the elevator pitch is to get the person to respond with an inquiry: "how?", or "tell me more" is what you want to hear. If you get an "humph", "that's nice" or similar disregarding comments, then you know you need to rethink your pitch. The more you tinker with it, the better it will get so don't be disheartened if your first attempts don't rock the boat for the potential customers.

You have now completed the first step in your Plan—defining your business. Make sure it is documented and backed up as you will need to make changes as you gain more business knowledge and market experience.

Start-up Resources

Now is a good time to think about what resources you will need to get the company started and what the requirements are likely to be for the first 12 months of operation. We can break resources down into 2 sub-components: startup needs and operational needs.

Start-up

Manpower resources. Will you need to employ additional staff for your business, and if so, do you require them from day one? Extra human resources mean extra finances. People cost money, even temporary staff, so unless you cannot manufacture your product because you lack the skills or, you expect a very active website and need the services of marketing or content writers, then I recommend that you try to hold off on employing staff until it is necessary. Maybe you can chain the family members to the oars and get them helping from time to time when the workload spikes.

I know this sounds obvious but when starting out it is imperative to keep your costs as low as possible so the occasional request for help from family and friends is needed.

I will talk more later in this book about of the complexities of bringing employees into a home business.

Production equipment. This only refers to those folks who will need equipment to manufacture their product. It could be as large and as technical as a lathe or pipe cutting machine or as simple as a cooker. But if you do not already have the equipment, you will need to factor this into your financial calculations. We will cover this aspect in the Financial Plan later, so I won't elaborate further at this stage.

Communication equipment. Being able to communicate effectively with your suppliers and customers is essential. To do this, you must have the right equipment: broadband or Wi-Fi connection, and a cell phone are the minimum requirements.

In my part of the world, broadband connections are expensive, slow and unreliable and thus Internet-based activities such as Skype discussions, attending webinars or creating podcasts with guests can be extremely difficult. There is nothing worse than having your Skype connection with a customer freeze or go down just as you are about to seal the deal.

For those outside the so-called First World or developed nations, Internet connectivity can be a troublesome aspect so do the homework and find out what you can and can't achieve. The reliability factor can have an influence on your choice of business.

Operational Requirements

These are things that you will need on a day-to-day basis for your business.

Examples of this would include office requisites, transport, and consumables used in production [but not the raw materials].

Office requisites would include all those items that you will need to operate your home business office and include hardware such as computers, printers, scanners, desk, chair, and filing cabinets. Again, we will discuss much of this in the Financial Plan so I will not belabor the point other than to say don't splash out in the beginning. Make use of what you already have and add the other items as the business grows.

Some thoughts on your office space or working area. Ideally, you want to have a dedicated room where you can set up a workspace that provides you with not only all the tools you require to operate your company but also seclusion from the rest of the household. This is often easier said than done and it is not uncommon to find home business owners running their business from the coffee table in the lounge or the kitchen table.

However, your circumstances dictate your workspace and the concept of working from home needs the commitment and involvement of everyone living in the same space. You need to limit the impact on the daily comings and goings of the other residents into your work space and they need to allow you space and solitude to conduct your business. Difficult at the best of times.

Step 2 – The Product

Time now to delve deeper into the nature of your product. It is important to understand that this is the product that the public will see on day one and could well be a much-shortened version of what you envisage the ultimate product, or range of products, will look like. But you need to start somewhere and at this early stage, simple is smartest.

Depending on the business you have decided to launch, your product will fall within one of the following categorizations:

Make to sell

In this instance you will offer a tangible product for sale. Your product will be sold either from your business premises, your e-commerce site or through a selection of outlets owned by others. Examples would include, cupcakes, artworks, security gates, curios, clothes, eBooks, and training courses.

Provide an on-site service

By "on-site", I mean that the service you provide will, in most cases, be carried out at the customer's premises. This includes IT support, plumbers, electricians, health practitioners, business consultants, and the like. You will offer your knowledge and expertize to perform a service at your customer's premises. Sometimes, you will be required to offer your customers a "supply and install" service.

What this means is that while you are repairing a computer, you may have to replace some components which you will "buy and resell" to the customer as part of the overall service. You could also offer goods associated with the service you provide; for example, as an IT technician, you could also sell PC peripherals.

Provide an offsite service

Although you may work at a customer's premises from time to time, you will do the majority of the work at home. These services include website design, accountants, tax experts, business and lifestyle consultants are just some examples. As with the on-site services you could also offer associated products, as a tax consultant you could compile and sell a booklet explaining the tax benefits entitled to a small business owner.

DEFINING THE PRODUCT

Unless you clearly understand what your offering entails, you cannot expect the general consumer to assume what it is and then buy it. In the early stages of your new business **simple is smart**. Don't over complicate the product or service. Offer your best versions first. Start small and grow your product range as you increase and secure your customer base.

You also need to think about how you intend to present your product and what features you will add to it to make it different from your competitors' product. A good place to start is to get out there in the market place and see how others are doing it.

Using the above categorizations let's look at how to best define your product.

Make to sell

Let's imagine you are going to make and sell cupcakes. You have probably been baking cupcakes for years and can showcase a wide variety of flavors, toppings, and designs but for the purpose of launching your business, you may want to decide on a limited number to begin with. For instance, the choice may go to those flavors that are frequently requested by family and friends. These are more likely to sell to new customers as they have passed the "proof is in the eating" test.

Next, how do you intend to package them? Individually, in packs of 4 or 6? Will you use special trays or simply pack them in paper cups? Will you want to advertise your company on the packaging or only have a sticker with your company name and contact number? The presentation can have a profound effect on the consumers choice, so think carefully about the look of your product when it is on the shelf.

Lastly, give serious consideration as to how you can make your product unique or stand out from the crowd of your competitor's products. How does the competitions product stack up against yours? Are there any "value add" aspects to the competitor's product? For example, do they pack their products in reusable trays? Do they offer volume discounts – buy 10 and get 2 FREE.

Provide an on-site service.

Being an on-site service provider does have its problems. For example, as a plumber you may be called out to attend to what appears to be a routine problem only to find on further examination that the problem is far more complex than you initially anticipated. You need to be geared up to handle whatever crises the customer is experiencing.

Know what you can do and what you can't. If your knowledge of geyser repairs is shaky, don't offer to repair them. Offer only what you know you can provide. Make a list of possible jobs that you could be called out for and eliminate those you are not comfortable taking on. Will you only provide repair services or are you able to offer new installations?

Will you offer after hours and weekend services or provide free quotations perhaps, or offer a discount for work over a certain value? Find out what your competitors are doing and offering. Clearly define what it is you are going to offer.

As a consumer, who has frequently had to call in a plumber, I would rather be told that fixing the geyser is not within their expertize than have a mess made of the job and still have to call another plumber to fix it.

As already highlighted, you need to find a way to make your service stand out from the competitors.

Provide an offsite service

As with the onsite services you need to be clear as to what you offer, how you will provide the service and what the customer will get for their money. If you are a tax consultant, I would need to know, for example, whether you provide consultancy support for personal tax only or do you also aid home and small businesses?

Confused customers tend to go elsewhere for what they need.

PRICING THE PRODUCT

Disclaimer: I am not an accountant, nor do I profess to be an expert in the field. The suggestions below are nothing other than that, suggestions. This section provides you with a rudimentary guideline which will enable you to calculate a reasonably accurate "ballpark" cost for your product. This will assist you in determining your potential selling price. I recommend that you refer your calculations to your accountant for verification if only to ensure that they are acceptable for audit and tax remittance purposes.

A common conundrum that faces new home business start-ups is how to price their products or services.

There is the tendency to look at what the competition charges and then offer their product at a slightly lower price hoping to attract customers. A problem with this approach is that your selling price may not cover your costs to produce your product. Your dilemma is that if you price too high consumers, who don't know your company, will remain with their existing supplier and if you price too low, the market place could interpret your product as being "cheap junk".

The lower the selling price, the smaller the profit margin and therefore the greater the pressure on your cost components. This means your focus will be on trying to drive down your cost elements that make up your basic product price, which is not a bad strategy in the big scheme of things, but as a new start-up, it could ultimately result in lower quality.

The first step in determining your selling price is to calculate the total cost associated with producing or providing a single product or a batch of products. If you are manufacturing or reselling someone else's product, this may be a substantial figure. The cost of providing a financial consulting service may only entail the cost of your time. Irrespective of what you will sell, you need to do the math.

Cost components that make up your Product Cost price

There are 5 cost components which will impact on your selling price. These are the cost contributors which will enable you to calculate the Cost Price of your product, in other words, what it will cost you to make one complete product or provide one service. I have taken the liberty of distorting the correct descriptions for some components for the sake of simplicity. My apologies to all you financial gurus.

They are:

All the costs associated with making one product or a batch of products *[sometimes referred to as Direct Costs].* For example, manufacturing one chair or making a batch of 24 cupcakes. These costs include all the raw materials or ingredients, consumables, utilities [see note below], delivery costs, the marketing and selling costs and if you intend to employ labor [maybe a temp to fulfill a specific task], that cost. Or it could just be your hourly rate. If you will be making more than one TYPE of product, then you will need to calculate for each type, apportioning out costs as applicable.

Some industry examples:

Making a product—which could be anything from furniture, clothing, pastries, writing a "how to" eBook, artwork, seedlings or buying someone else's product and reselling it.

Providing an on-site service—as a plumber, electrician or IT repairs. Your cost is most likely going to be predominately labor, the charge per hour when you are on site. To this, you may add parts and components, but you will sell these on a "cost-plus basis", in other words, the cost you paid to buy the part plus the mark-up you add.

These are often unknown at the outset of each job so add them on completion.

The provision of offsite services is commonly associated with consultants: accounting, tax, HR, lifestyle, website design and support, beauticians and health consultants are some examples. Again, the hourly charge will be the primary component but then there may be products or consumables that are consumed in providing the service. For example, where you use a sub-consultant their hourly rate would be included. Let's say you build web sites, but your HTML coding is, at the moment shaky; so, you use a coding expert to help with a specific build. You could either charge your customer the sub-consultant's cost, as quoted to you [and so recover your costs], or include a portion of their total cost in your hourly rate. So, if they charge you 100 and you will do 20 hours work on the design, you would divide the 100 by 20 and add the 5 to your hourly rate. Some service providers will add a "management fee" to sub-consultants' costs; the 5 would be say 6, the extra being your time to manage the sub-consultant.

Note: Service providers can opt to either charge per hour and then add on the cost of any replacement parts supplied or quote a "lump sum price" for a job. This second option is only offered when it is possible to calculate the time it will take to complete the work and prior knowledge of what parts or consumables they will need.

The costs associated with running the business [also known as Fixed and/or Indirect Costs] apply whether you made a million products or none. These would include any rent, utilities [see note below], rental or lease costs of equipment, internet connectivity costs, etc.

Your salary

Any financial obligations for example, repayment of a loan.

Start-up or capital cost. This is the equipment that you purchased to either produce your product or to provide infrastructure to run the business. Depending on the Generally Accepted Accounting Principles and legislature governing tax deductions for businesses applicable in your country, there may be legitimate ways in which you can "write off" these expenses against company tax over time or through other legal accounting adjustments.

Please discuss this with your accountant or tax advisor. The rules and laws in some countries are complex and confusing so before trying to "duck the system" find out what avenues are open to you.

You could also recover your start-up costs by including them in your product price, obviously not the total cost against one product, but amortized over the number of products or services sold in say, one year. If you calculate your product price to be 10, you anticipate selling a 100 per month for the first 12 months [1200 in total] and your start-up cost is 500, you could add 0.42 to the selling price of each product and recover your start-up costs in year 1.

CALCULATING THE PRODUCT PRICE

The easiest way [other than telling your accountant to do it for you] is to start by picking a time period, let's use a month for this example, and calculate all the expenses you will incur in that given period. Using a spreadsheet is the ideal tool for this purpose. This will give you the total cost for everything you need to make one product or provide one service for one month.

Let's start by adding up the cost for ONE month of the following cost components:

The operating cost for the company for one month.

Your monthly salary.

All your monthly financial obligations.

The aggregate of all these components is your total MONTHLY cost to run your business **without producing a single product**.

Now calculate the cost to produce ONE product or batch of products or one service [The Direct Cost, as explained in the previous section]. Added to the total monthly costs to run your business will provide you with the minimum SELLING price of your one product or service assuming you only sold one product and wanted to recover all your costs—the breakeven point. What is excluded from this calculation is your mark-up or PROFIT. But this number is unrealistic unless you manufacture gold bars. You need to be making more than a single product each month if you intend to be profitable. To make it realistic, you will need to estimate your monthly production to begin with.

If you intend to produce 100 widgets in a month, then the monthly direct cost would be the cost to make one product x 100. Now your total monthly cost will look something like this:

cost to make one widget x 100;

operating costs for one month;

salary;

all your monthly financial obligations, and

inclusion of any start-up cost per product portion.

This aggregate is the TOTAL COST per month to make 100 widgets. To determine your break-even price per product, divide the total cost by 100. To this figure a "mark-up" needs to be added to the price; this represents the profit you think is fair and relevant.

You now have an estimated selling price that you can adjust up or down depending on what the next steps in the research process reveal.

How to determine the right selling price

Being able to identify the right price at which to enter the market depends very much on the quality of your research and the effectiveness of your pre-launch marketing.

How much should your profit be?

There are various "standards" or guidelines as to what companies within certain industries use as the benchmark profit margin. As a new kid on the block, your profit margin will depend on what your competitors are charging and what the market sector will accept as a fair price. Assuming that in both cases the selling prices exceed the cost to make your product.

Let me explain. You anticipate selling 100 trays of 6 cupcakes per month. If the highest price for a tray of 6 cupcakes in your intended market is 6, and the lowest is 5, you will have to pitch somewhere in between, say 5.50 to begin with. If your Total Cost to produce a tray is 4.50, you will be able to add a mark-up of 1. Turnover per month, based on a monthly output of 100 trays, will be 550, total cost 450 and profit 100.

When trying to assess what profit to add to your cost here are some considerations.

Using the above prices—if your cost element adds up to 5.50 or thereabouts you need to re-examine your cost components. Maybe change the packaging for a cheaper plastic or opt for a less expensive tray. Many new home business owners exclude a salary for themselves until the business turns a profit, or at least take a very nominal one. This is very doable if you have alternative income that covers the home expenses. If you can refrain from taking a salary, it will have a meaningful impact on the cost calculation.

You may have to experiment with the profit margin until you can identify a price acceptable to the market place. Remember it is easier to drop your price than to raise it.

Once you enter the market, gauge the reaction of your competitors. Where there is limited competition, your entry could have a noticeable effect and larger suppliers may attempt to edge you out by offering discounts to undercut your price. This is where the "value add" to your product will pay dividends. If customers perceive that the total value they will receive for their purchase exceeds the higher price, they could be enticed into sampling your product.

Where would I price?

I would opt for the upper half of the pricing bracket. If the highest price is 6 and the lowest 5, I would initially price between 5.50 and say 5.80. This allows me the option to lower my price to entice new customers through "special offers" giving the impression of a bargain. Consumers love bargains.

What will the market accept?

Research the top and bottom end of the pricing spectrums in the market. What influences does the market have on product prices— is it impacted by weather changes, are there seasonal trends, is there an over or under supply? Have there been any surprises, for example, did the market react demonstrably when there was a new entrant?

The more you know about what the market finds acceptable the easier it will be to peg an acceptable price from the outset. The less you have to juggle with your price, the better.

What about competitors?

Competition is healthy; it at least proves that folks are buying what you are hoping to sell.

As with the previous paragraph, you need to research your competition.

What prices do they offer, are there significant price differences, and if so, why?

Is there a link between the size of the competitor and the product price? Possibly. Larger companies tend to have higher overheads which they need to be recoup resulting in a higher price than that of a smaller business. However, this is often offset by added benefits such as product guarantees, free deliveries and occasional discounts and customer's preferences to purchase from "more reputable" sources.

Crucially you must compare apples to apples when looking at the competitors pricing otherwise you may get a skewed view of the competition.

Over the years, consumers have become even more price conscious. Online stores have increased their options and made it more difficult for traditional suppliers to compete. This has resulted in consumers becoming more astute in their choices. The average consumer can shop around and will do so until they can get the best value for their money. This means they are looking for more than just the lowest price. The consumer of today is looking for the best VALUE for their purchase to use an old phrase, "the best bang for their buck".

To meet this demand, suppliers need to offer their best VALUE PROPOSITIONS. This goes beyond having the cheapest or best price for an article. The product needs to offer more than what is in the packaging. It needs to be differentiated from the competition's offer. This value add may include an extended guarantee or the provision of a free service attached to the product, for example, free training.

If the consumer perceives a greater value in the product, the price can become incidental; price is no longer the ruling factor. The trick is how to convey those benefits of your value proposition to the consumer. This calls for innovative strategies when presenting your product to the market place.

"Customers need to perceive the benefits of what you're selling— the higher the perceived benefit [all other things being equal], the more you can charge."—Dileep Rao, Get It Right: Pricing Strategies That Work

There are certain markets where the selling price is dictated by precedent. The more niche specific your product is the more inflexible you can be with your pricing as there will be less competitors to allow you to compare against. In order to be competitive when you enter the market you may be forced to align your selling price with what is deemed the industry norm.

The key is understanding the market, and in particular, the segment in which you intend to offer your product. Know what the competition is offering and more importantly, what your targeted customer needs. Finding the right slot for your price will take some trial and error but as you get to understand your customer base better and can identify the value they are looking for, the quicker your pricing strategy will fall into place.

And don't forget—a top quality product or service is something the consumer expects and the trick with proving quality is consistency.

Step 3 – The Marketing Plan

Irrespective of whether you intend to sell cookies, repair cars, provide a plumbing service, write books or sell paintings from a website; if people don't know about you, you are unlikely to sell anything. The chances of being "discovered" by consumers or other business entities are remote.

Marketing is an ever-ongoing part of being a business owner; if no one knows you exist, you will not sell. This means you must get into people's faces and tell them why buying your product is the best thing they will have done that day.

This step is about how you go about putting your new home business on the map, whether it is in your local community or worldwide through your website. But first let me share some background as to what marketing, and its close cousin, selling is about.

Marketing versus Selling

Although interchangeable in the small business environment, there is a difference. As a home business owner, you will probably fulfill both roles, that is until your company grows to the extent where you can allocate specific marketing or sales tasks to your expanding workforce. For clarity on the differences, **Diffen.com** explains the differences:

"The typical goal of marketing is to generate interest in the product and create leads or prospects. Marketing activities include:

consumer research to identify the needs of the customer's

product development—designing innovative products to meet existing or latent needs

advertising the products to raise awareness and build the brand.

pricing products and services to maximize long-term revenue.

On the other hand, sales activities are focused on converting prospects to actual paying customers. Sales involves directly interacting with the prospects to persuade them to purchase the product.

Marketing thus tends to focus on the general population [or, in any case, a large set of people] whereas sales tends to focus on individuals or a small group of prospects."

The difference as you need to understand it for now is that Marketing is about developing the plan—**the where and how** you will take your product to market. Sales will refer to your delivery method—having your product in the right place, at the right time and at the right price, all of which will entice the customer to purchase it.

For example:

Identifying the local weekly town market as the where and how you will offer your cupcakes for sale is the marketing element. Your physical presence on market day, along with a truckload of cupcakes, is the sales bit.

But as I mentioned before, don't get hung up on the definitions for now and whether you use the terms interchangeably at this early stage will not affect your business.

What is important is that you develop a plan, and for our purpose, we will call it your Marketing Plan. This plan will define:

1) what the end product will look like and which price best suits which market;
2) a profile for your intended customer;
3) what markets you intend to penetrate, and
4) how you intend to tell the market place about your product or your brand.

Each one of these elements will require research and the better your research, the better your plan. The good news is you have already done a sizable chunk of the research - when you decided on what type of business you would launch, as discussed in Part 1. But let's address each element and make sure all the blocks are checked. Before we do that, let's first look at YOU and how this marketing and selling lark will sit with you.

You the marketer

Marketing your company is as much about selling yourself as it is about selling your products or services. The fact is that as a new home-based business owner, YOU are the company and everything that the company IS will be exhibited by your personal demeanor and presentation.

It is for this very reason that you will recall me harping on about making sure you are the very best you can be at what you offer. In Part 1, I dedicated substantial space to talking about knowing what your strengths and weaknesses were and what you were good at compared to those activities or interests that fell into the "ham-fisted" classification. Marketing and selling are a point in case.

Arriving at a customer's house to repair a leaking pipe with a copy of the "Dummies Guide to Plumbing" tucked under your arm is unlikely to instill a sense of confidence in the house owner. Similarly advising someone on your website that you will "get back to them" in response to their website design query [as you frantically plow through Google looking for the answer] will probably result in the person taking their business elsewhere.

Being professional is a way of marketing your business.

The world is what it is and consumers, with their sometimes-peculiar assessments of how and where they will spend their money are the ultimate user and buyer of your service or product and it is them you will need to impress. And until you can afford the luxury of employees to do it for you, you are all you have.

You may wonder where I am going with all of this. Let me explain. I had a partner who was a crappy salesman in a one-on-one situation, and no, I have no idea why. He could do amazing formal presentations and could convince a CEO and a board of directors to buy almost anything. But with convincing someone at the counter to buy our widget, things didn't always go to plan. Not a people person you say, probably right and if so, it is almost a certainty that the potential customer picked up on that. So, no matter how great our product was it was the way he presented it to the potential customer that appears to have negatively influenced the individuals final purchasing consideration.

Yes, I am generalizing, but it is important to understand what you can and can't do. If you can sell sand to Egyptians, get out there and make money, but if dealing with people and the thought of trying to convince them that your homemade chocolates are on a par with the best chocolate in the world turns you nauseous, then you need to develop a Plan B.

We will talk about this handicap in some detail, because it is one I can associate with. But if selling is a problem, you need to understand the difference between marketing and selling. You may have what it takes to plan and design the marketing plan, but you will need to find a salesperson to get your goodies sold, or vice versa.

CREATING THE MARKETING PLAN

But let's get back to the Marketing Plan.

The Product and Pricing

In Step 2—The Product, we spent a whole heap of time talking about product selection and pricing parameters and therefore I will not labor the point any further suffice to say that the type or kind of product you offer will, to a large degree, dictate the look and feel of your marketing plan.

Potential Customer Profile

Your potential customer base will be a natural consequence of your product selection.

The greater the need the larger the customer base; the more specialized the product the smaller the market. For example, if you offer a wide range of cookies you will attract a broad spectrum of customers, however if you sell cupcakes only, you're likely to have a smaller customer base.

This opinion may fly in the face of all the experts' advice about identifying your ideal customer and designing your marketing drive and sales pitch to match that profile, but I believe that when you start out as a home business owner, assuming like most of us that finances are in short supply, being too specific and selective can be a negative. Again, I generalize, but unless you have a very niche specific product, maybe a coffee mug for astronauts that won't float around the cabin, my advice is to go broad with your marketing plan. When you first start out, tell as many people and companies about who you are and what product or service you offer.

As sales escalate and you can identify your "type of customer", you will have time to be more selective and targeted in your marketing efforts.

Market Penetration

Before deciding on how you intend to capture your first customer, and many more thereafter, you must decide on the mechanisms you will use to announce your presence in the market place, but you first need to identify the markets you intend to gain access to.

Although I indicated that going wide with your marketing drive was a good way to start, common sense should prevail.

Every owner of a property that has running water and a sewage system would be a potential customer if you're a plumber. Offering female beauty products to members of the men's only fishing club may not be as rewarding [well, maybe not].

Similarly, if web design is your specialty, contacting well-established sites that have been catering for tens of thousands of subscribers for years, and offering to redesign their website is just plain weird.

The nature of your product or service will dictate the market you will aim at. So, when applying the broad-brush approach, do so within the market that has a proven track record for the demand for your product or service.

If you offer a tangible product or service, you will also need to consider your ability to access the markets. If you do not have transport, it is pointless earmarking a neighboring town as a potential market.

Advertising

If you have the money use a professional advertising agency. Alternatively, you could have a crack at creating your own advert using one of the many free software packages available online. But remember, a bad advert could be worse than no advertising at all.

If you employ an agency check on the following:

- what does each publication charge;
- what are the sizes of adverts and where do they appear on the pages;
- what is the reach of each publication or website [how many subscribers do they have], and
- determine the publications applicability to your industry and how many displays do you get per payment?

Advertising on social media, if done correctly, can be rewarding but it can also be expensive. Before spending money on social media platforms make sure that the adverts will target your intended market. Pointless having a global reach with your Facebook ad if you only selling to your local community.

Be miserly with your money and don't hesitate to get feedback from folks who have used the publications or platforms as to their success ratings.

Marketing opportunities

Here is a suggested list of potential markets which is not exhaustive, so be innovative in your endeavors and always be on the lookout for unique and untapped markets.

Where your target market is local, and you offer a tangible product or a service

As a home-based business offering a tangible product, you rarely have a "storefront" where customers can view your products and make selections and maybe you really don't want strangers coming to your home, even if it is to spend money. So, you need to get very smart in the way you attract buyers.

If you don't have a storefront, and you won't be delivering directly to your customers, then you need to find one and this may mean offering your products through third party outlets such as stores or coffee shops as examples. When selling through third parties, they will generally place your products on display, thus attracting the interest of buyers. However, depending on the arrangement you have with the third party, you still want to be alerting potential customers about your product and steering them towards the purchase points.

Use all the social media tools that are available to you. Don't overdo the selling but keep up a consistent flow of information and product news.

Approach family and friends. Although you may be reluctant to involve family and friends, they, along with all their "besties" and not so "besties", can be a very potent ally for spreading the word. Comments on Facebook pages or through Twitter to their followers [in your area if applicable] can have positive results, so don't be afraid to ask for their help. Get all your other contacts and associates to do the same on your behalf.

Your partner's place of employment. Be careful with this one, but if your partner works for a company or corporate with lots of potential buyers for your product, ask him or her if the company will allow them to market your wares in the office. There is nothing wrong with them "mentioning" your new venture to co-workers over a cup of coffee or at the water dispenser, obviously with no intention of actively pushing your product, of course not.

Your current employer. As with your partner's employer, I advise some caution. It will become obvious once you have tendered your resignation, what your intended plans are so when convenient, expand on your ideas and intentions with co-workers and if the reception is positive ask them to "spread the gospel" to all and sundry. Depending on what your new business is all about, there may be an opportunity to sell your wares to your current employer. If so, approach your line manager and ascertain what the company rules are—I have worked for an employer whose rules stated that previous employees were not permitted to tender for company business until 6 months after resigning. If there are no trading restrictions, ask to meet with the company buyer and chat to him or her about your new company and ask if you can be added to the list of suppliers—don't expect special treatment because you are an employee.

Join other social media platforms that are more business orientated, such as LinkedIn, Google+ and industry forums. There are groups or communities on these sites, which fall into two main categories: small business information and those associated with your product or service.

Although they will cater for folks from all over the world and therefore may lack local suitability, they provide a very informative source of up-to-date information on what other small and home business owners are doing and what is happening, generally, in your chosen industry.

Please exercise caution here. Although most Groups and Communities on these platforms will tolerate advertising, don't flog your company to death. Use the opportunities to discuss your product in the industry's context, ask questions, share tips and develop a rapport with the other members and build a following. If you are already talking to them, telling them you have just launched your website will generate more interest than if you go in with product banners and adverts blazing on day one.

If you are not already a member, join your local business chamber and industry associations. Many of these organizations offer platforms for new members to introduce themselves and their products or services. Introductions may take the form of a 5-minute presentation at a weekly or monthly meeting or dinner or a short article in their publications. Take full advantage of any support provided.

Look to find ways to tell your local community about your company. Be liberal in handing out your business cards—if it moves, give it a card, likewise with your flyers and brochures. Shopping malls, school functions, local weekend markets, and sporting events are good places to start but make sure you have the agreement of the complex or event managers to do so but please, do not stick flyers and brochures on car windshields—it is extremely annoying to the car owner.

Check with your local postal delivery service. In my country, for a small fee, they will insert flyers into all the post boxes in your area. You can also coerce or incentivize family members to drop off literature in homeowners post boxes. I know, you are bordering on becoming a spammer, but if you limit this exercise to once before launch and once afterward, I'm sure you will be forgiven.

If you have a local newspaper or community newsletter, contact the editor and find out if there is an opportunity to insert a small advert or a flyer. In many communities, they deliver these publications to homes and local businesses on a weekly or monthly basis. There may also be an opportunity to write an article for them using your expertize on the topic for example, if you are an accountant, writing a short piece about tax saving tips could be very well received.

Approaching local businesses requires a different tack. Find out if there is a dedicated buyer at the company and meet with him or her. Prepare a one-page letter [on your letterhead showing all your contact details] introducing both the company and your products. Make sure you point out that you are a home-based business and give some indication of what volumes of product you could supply, in say a month, and specify what your quality specifications will be. There is a pro and con argument to including a price. I know, from bitter experience, that unethical buyers in some companies may share your price with your competition. On the other hand, revealing your price will let the buyer know immediately if you are competitive or not. Some buyers and company owners may help by telling you whether your price is "ballpark", which is very helpful. If you are in two minds as to what to do, include an "indicative price" subject to confirmation on placing orders.

When approaching companies, it will be worthwhile to find out whether they have a program aimed at assisting SME/B's. If so, find out who manages the program and meet with them.

Should you have a permanent online presence, such as a website? This depends on what you sell and you not having a storefront to attract street side traffic. But keep in mind that the statistics tell us that consumers are making greater use of mobile devices when searching for goods and services, even locally [this varies depending on which country you live in], so you will need to do the research to establish if having an online presence will bring results. In my part of the world, for example, there are several web sites that specialize in free advertising for small businesses.

Using online directories where you can advertise your business is another option.

Where you offer an online product or service

Contrary to what I was led to believe when I started in business, I see no major differences between how you market your online business to that of a brick and mortar business. It all comes down to your profile in the market place, the more people who know about your website the better, whether they find you online or you hand out a business card at the local supermarket makes no difference. With this in mind I would recommend that you make use of all the suggestions listed in the "tangible products" section, adapting them as necessary.

Your website will be your storefront and therefore that is where you need the customers to go, not to your home office. Your website address becomes your contact number as opposed to a telephone or cell number and therefore, it should appear in BIG BOLD letters on all your literature.

PRE-LAUNCH MARKETING

Unlike your marketing plan and ongoing campaigns, pre-launch marketing is a "once off", big bang approach to telling as many potential customers that you are about to enter the market with your product or service, BEFORE you launch the company.

Deciding when to tell the public about your arrival in the market will depend very much on the product or service you will be offering. Once you have set a date to launch your company, you then need to plan backwards to decide on how long before launch date you should tell people about your company. If you are selling services or consumables, you don't need that long a pre-launch period; perhaps several weeks would be enough.

While your ongoing marketing campaigns, after you launch, will be well researched and the target markets identified that will offer the greatest return on your investment, your pre-launch drive should be a scatter-shot approach - as broad and as wide as you can go. The more people who know about you, the greater the chances of securing pre-launch orders.

Don't start marketing your wares until the company is registered and you have a reasonable amount of sample products [if applicable]. Also make sure you have a good stockpile of business cards, and if you intend to use them, flyers or one-page brochures talking about your company launch and the product/s.

If finances permit, publishing paid for notifications in the local press and on social media is a good way to go but as with most new home business start-ups, this might not be feasible so using the suggested targets listed above for your marketing plan will be a good start.

BRANDING

The branding or brands that we see in our everyday life are often associated with large corporations, and we assume it is a marketing technique that only they can afford. Not so. Many of the household names we see today started out as home-based businesses and include such famous names as Facebook, Harley Davidson, Apple, Amazon, and Lotus cars.

There is no reason you can't brand your product, service or even your company name.

What is branding?

WhatIs.com explains it:

"A brand is a product, service, or concept that is publicly distinguished from other products, services, or concepts so that it can be easily communicated and usually marketed. A brand name is the name of the distinctive product, service, or concept.

Branding is the process of creating and disseminating the brand name. Branding can be applied to the entire corporate identity as well as to individual product and service names. Brands are usually protected from use by others by securing a trademark or service mark from an authorized agency, usually a government agency."

David Ogilvy, advertising copywriter, and ad agency founder defines it thus:

"The intangible sum of a product's attributes: its name, packaging, and price, its history, its reputation, and the way it's advertised."

As you can see it is more than just a name or logo, it is about the business: the product performance, after sales service, customer support, market relationships and performance history, and as you start out, it is also about you and how you represent your company and products.

Many companies brand their products by attaining a Trademark to protect the name or graphic and if you intend to go this route, I strongly recommend that you seek legal advice.

If you would like to understand more about branding and what it can do for your product, here are a series of articles published on the **Forbes** website and a **Guide on Quicksprout** which are must reads.

DOCUMENTING THE PLAN AND OTHER CONSIDERATIONS

Documenting the Marketing Plan

Now that you are aware of the options available to a home business owner to make your presence known in the intended market, you need to draft an action plan.

Decide on how you intend to market your business, from pre-launch through each month for the first 12 months. Write it down.

Determine if there will be any costs associated with each element and record them – you will need them for your financial plan.

Decide on how you will sell your product. Will you go door-to-door, rely on interactive web sites or will you approach intermediaries to sell on your behalf. Write it down.

It is also an idea to put some thought to when you will do your marketing or advertising. You may choose to "hit the market place" first thing in the morning or perhaps you prefer to do it in the evenings. Set a fixed time aside each day – you can always adjust it as circumstances permit but get into the habit of allocating some time each day to market your business.

Cold Calling

The bane of many a new business owner. I hate cold calling and I know that many other business owners experience the same heart-stopping sensation when they need to pick up a phone and call a total stranger and try and convince them to spend their money with another total stranger.

Is there a formula to circumvent cold calling? Not that I know of.

But here is one way I have found which helps and is perhaps slightly less stressful.

I contact all my friends, family members, and business contacts and associates and ask them to recommend at least 2 people who they believe would be interested in what I have to offer. They must personally know the recommended individuals and agree that I can use their name when calling. My cold call will then go something like this:

"Hi there [or whatever greeting is acceptable in your part of the world] my name is ..... and I am the owner of .... Company. Your friend/relative/contact gave me your name as he/she believes you may be interested in what my company offers."

If your contact has already bought or used your product, I would include that fact.

I then follow up with the "elevator pitch".

Hope this helps.

Customer Service and support

Irrespective of the type of business you launch, without customers you're not going to survive for very long. So, finding and retaining customers is fundamentally what your marketing plan is aiming to achieve.

And as I've already alluded to, repeat customers are your initial goal- folks who will keep coming back for your product and hopefully are telling others how great it is!

But to enjoy this windfall you need to have a customer service policy in place. And it is much more than just being polite or quick to respond. It must encompass all the attributes of your business: quality, delivery, pricing and after-sales service. Each customer needs to feel as though they are your one and only customer and are being treated accordingly.

Your product or service quality must remain consistently high and if a product or service fails your own high standard for the quality test; you must have a remedy in place. How will you respond to customer complaints or product returns? Will you replace the product or refund the customer [assuming the complaint is legitimate] or will you adopt a "purchase at your own risk" approach?

Talk to your customers, they are the best gauge of how your company is perceived in the marketplace and don't be afraid to publicize your customer service policy. Customers want to know that quality is as important to you as it is to them.

Here are some facts that highlight the importance of customer care and satisfaction.

The primary reason why customers will stop buying from your company is dissatisfaction resulting from a lack of interest shown by the company. A 2019 survey done by **Small Biz Trends** showed that **82 percent of consumers** in the United States said they stopped doing business with a company due to a poor customer experience. To the consumer the dissatisfaction can be as simple as a complaint that is ignored or lack of follow-up when problems are highlighted with service issues or maybe as innocuous as an unanswered email. The cause is simply a bad or indifferent attitude by the owner and employees of the company towards the customer. Happened to you? I'm sure it has, and I also bet you didn't go back to the company.

Just to rub it in here are some other stats from the same survey:

- *companies lose 71 percent of consumers due to poor customer service;*
- *68 percent of customers leave you because they perceive you are indifferent to them;*
- *60 to 70 percent of customers will do business with a company again if it deals with a customer service issue fairly even if the result is not in their favor;*
- *47 percent of customers would take their business to a competitor within a day of experiencing poor customer service; and*

- *66 percent of consumers who switched brands did so because of poor service.*

A quote from Richard Lazazerra founder of A Better Lemonade Stand. *"It's cheaper to get past customers to purchase again than it is to find new customers."* By some estimates as much as 5 times cheaper. Depending on the industry, there is a 60-70% chance of success selling to an existing customer whereas only around 10-20% of new customers will purchase. You are also more likely to get a second chance to remedy a problem with a loyal customer than you would with a first-time buyer.

It has also been estimated that as much as 65% of a company's business will come from loyal customers.

Looking after your customers and ensuring that the once-off customer comes back for more [and becomes the repeat customer] is the most aggressive marketing and sales strategy you can use.

Happy customers tell other people about your company and they, if recipients of the same good service, will tell others and before you know it, your company is the talk of the town. Word of mouth marketing by customers is the cheapest and most credible advertising you can have.

Customer care is a very serious business, so learn as much as you can as soon as you can.

Step 4 - The Growth Plan

During the planning phase of your business, you may consider it somewhat premature to be thinking about the potential growth of your company and you may be right. However, if it is your intention to take your business beyond a home office, then you need to give some thought to how you envisage the business will look in say, one years' time, three years' time and possibly even 5 years from now.

There will come a time in the life cycle of your home business when you will need to give serious consideration as to whether you want a larger business or if you are happy where you are.

Most business consultants will tell you that you need to provide for a growth plan in your formal Business Plan, this is true if you are trying to raise start-up capital or looking to engage a partner for the business.

But there is nothing in the rulebook that says you must expand.

There are many so-called "lifestyle" home business owners, sometimes called a "mom and pop" business, who have built up their business to a point where it provides a comfortable lifestyle. They love what they do and feel comfortable with the workload which allows an equitable balance between work and family.

Absolutely nothing wrong with this scenario. However, stagnation can begin to creep in.

Let's look at this scenario. You've noticed that your "mom and pop" business is just not showing the same profitability as before, and although your regular customers keep coming back you are not increasing your new customer base. You're finding it difficult to increase your product price, costs are increasing annually, and your profit margins are getting squeezed. In simple terms, your business is stagnating, and going nowhere.

This form of stagnation can very quickly become apparent where the owner provides a one-on-one service to his or her customers. Accountants, tax consultants, and health care professionals come to mind. They provide a single service to a customer, which is usually labor intensive. They prepare month-end accounts for a client or a specific health care treatment to a patient—all of which takes up hours within a day, and there are only so many hours in a working day. In short, the number of customers they can service is limited to the number of hours in a working day. They are unable to expand simply because they do not have the available time to take on new customers—their output capacity ceiling has been reached.

This may force you into a decision whether to expand or sell out.

Expansion plans for your business

With developing the growth plan for your business, everything is theoretical at this early stage. If you can declare from the outset that you have no intention of expanding your business and that being a "lifestyle" home business owner is your vision, then you need not put much thought into this component of your plan. I would suggest though that you do so—if only to satisfy yourself that not growing your business sometime in the future is what you want.

If however this business is something you have committed to for the long term and your intention is to leave a financially sound legacy, then now is the time to put a plan to all those long term dreams. As

I have mentioned before, when planning your business, think BIG and start SMALL.

Just a note on growing your home business. When the sales are up and the cash is flowing in, it's tempting to take the big swing and throw everything you have at expanding your business. To me growth for a small or home-based operation is a bit like trying to eat an elephant—the recommended serving size is "one bite at a time". As with your launch, start small and cement each stage of your growth and make sure it is not only viable but also sustainable. It is like using wooden blocks to build a tower—make sure each block is in place before you add another on top.

At this stage, the growth plan is a vision—where do you expect the business will be in say 3- and 5-years' time, and even beyond that? Yes, pie in the sky you may say but you will be the determinant of whether your business ends up being confined to the dream bin or becomes that very successful small or medium-sized business you always envisaged.

Creating a growth plan that is vague and more of a wish list than achievable goals is just a waste of time. You need to consider where you are aiming to take this business and so a lot of thought and research is needed. You will need to understand and be able to identify the signals or events that will alert you to the need to consider expansion. How they come about and what you need to be doing in the interim to cause them to happen.

The rest of this section on Growth is aimed at providing you some insights into what growing the business requires and how and when is the right time to implement.

With everything you have on your plate at the moment you may want to put this section into the "read later folder" and that's understandable, but remember, it is important to have some idea of what lies ahead, forewarned is forearmed. So, if you can, I would recommend you take the time to read through what follows.

When is the right time to expand?

Deciding on when to grow your business is governed by the circumstances in play at the time, and timing is what it is all about. Knowing when the time has arrived to expand your business will depend on certain milestones being achieved. The reasons for growth could be varied and may be because of you instigating a change or recognizing that the business has reached a plateau and it is time to think bigger.

There are various reasons for considering growing the business any one of which could persuade the owner to consider expanding the operation. These usually come about because the owner has identified certain **triggers or signals** emanating from the marketplace or from within the company, indicating that the time has arrived. Here are some of those triggers.

New product or new markets

Two obvious ways to expand your business are by either increasing your product range or variety or identifying new markets to enter. Sometimes this need to expand may be driven by customer demand or the emergence of an untapped market, for example, a new housing estate has just opened in your suburb and could do with your house cleaning services.

In order to maximize these opportunities, you will need to expand your operation. This could entail additional sales staff, extra storage space for inventory or spending money on increasing production.

It is important to note that the logic behind the decision to expand must be sound. Designing a new product for the market as a desperate attempt to save the business differs greatly from launching a new product as part of your growth plan. Simply having another string to your bow is not enough reason to commit money and resources to a growth strategy unless the return on your investment [ROI] justifies it. You need to ensure that there are other, supporting, developments taking place.

Cash flow

Your company has been reflecting a positive cash flow for a reasonable period and is trending towards continued positive performance as opposed to a short-term spike. This could be because of increasing sales in your existing market and your marketing efforts are bearing fruit.

You now need to put some thought as to where the most return can be achieved with the excess cash. Get your money working for you.

Growing customer base

Although many businesses rely on repeat customers to provide a substantial portion of their turnover, a growing new customer base is a good sign that it may be time to consider expanding your operation. Often this upswing in customers is a consequence of your regulars telling friends and colleagues about how great your product is.

Work overload

If you are struggling to keep pace with the growing demands of the business and assuming you are not overworked because of having to fix problems or fighting fires, it is another sign that growth may be the best solution.

Inquiries from outside your geographical area

An encouraging indicator that your marketing efforts and word-of-mouth advertising by your customers is paying dividends is when you start to receive inquiries from potential customers outside of your established geographical area.

Time to follow through and assess the viability of the new market.

DRAFTING THE GROWTH PLAN

The idea behind the growth plan is to chart the way forward for your business. But remember growth is not only about the business but includes your own personal growth as the owner.

If you have identified potential weaknesses or shortfalls in your business training and acumen, then this is the place to address how you intend to correct them and by when. Not only are you developing the Big Picture in terms of the future growth of the company, but you are also defining what YOU need to achieve and by when.

These are your milestones that will provide points of measurement for you to aim for.

A good idea when plotting your growth plan is to start at the end point—the ultimate vision of what you intend your company to be. You may start out as a cupcake supplier with an end goal of owning a bakery in 5 years' time.

Once you have the vision, you will need to work backward to identify each growth milestone and allocate a time frame in which you will achieve each milestone. This also applies to your own development.

Let's use the cupcake and bakery example.

When do you hope to launch your bakery by?

- Let's say in 5 years' time.

Where do you want the bakery to be situated?

- Opening in your own area is the plan to begin with.

What will be needed to open a bakery?

- Premises
- Equipment
- Vehicles
- Staff
- Funding

How long will be needed to get all these requirements in place before the launch of the bakery?

- Let's assume your best estimate is 12 months.

That means by year 4 you will need to begin:

- exploring financing options and approaching funders if necessary;
- begin identifying potential premises;
- identifying and pricing what equipment and vehicles you will need, and
- begin developing a human resources plan highlighting what your staff complement will look like and what qualifications everyone will be expected to have.

Let's explore the requirements you have listed.

What amount of finance will you need?

A quick look around in the "businesses for sale" section of your local press will provide a guideline as to what an existing bakery is selling for. Alternatively, you could chat with estate agents in your area and get an idea of the cost of different size business premises, either to rent or to buy. Whether to buy an existing business or start the bakery from scratch is a decision you will make once all the numbers have been assessed.

List the equipment you think a bakery would need and allocate rough guide costings.

Staffing the new bakery

Deciding on the staff complement is perhaps difficult at this early stage but if you can arrange it, contact other bakery owners and have a chat to him or her about the size of the staff, skill levels, total annual wage bill and anything else you think is pertinent. This is not as difficult as it sounds. I have undertaken similar exercises and have always found that small business owners are more than happy to share information with a start-up entrepreneur, provided you are not intending to start up across the road from them. It pays to think up a bit of a "cover story" [nothing underhand] as to why you need the information.

Internet searches for answers to specific problems may also prove enlightening.

Much of the information you gather at this stage will be irrelevant by the time you begin to actually expand but this exercise will provide you with a rough ballpark figure for the amount of funding you will need to have stashed away by year 4. This is also a good time to go back to your financial plan to see what your projected turnover will look like by year 4.

Your personal development

A re-look at your personal strengths and weaknesses analysis in Part 1 will give you a list of those skills and attributes that you have acknowledged as lacking but will be needed if the business is to succeed and then grow. You will need to decide which of these you will receive training for and which you will farm out to external resources.

Now you know what is needed in terms of your own development. Find out if there are any costs associated with improving your skills level and by when you will need to have acquired them.

Financial forecasts

Although at this stage all you have is a plan for the future, it may be necessary to include the financial forecasts for the Growth plan in your Financial Plan. For example, if you intend to allocate a percentage of your profits each year for future growth and hide the money under your mattress for when the day arrives, include this in your Financial Plan.

POSSIBLE ALTERNATIVES TO GROWTH STRATEGIES

The purpose of the above was not to ask you to now do an in-depth analysis of what you will need when you decide to grow your business but merely to get you to do some outlining of what it could entail. The detail will come when the right time arrives. My intention is to summarize what is required at this early stage in terms of *planning for your growth* so that this very important element of your business plan is not ignored or forgotten.

As a final thought. Growing your business is not a pre-requisite; there is another option.

Improving your business rather than increasing the size.

The idea here is about doing things smarter and being more efficient. The changes you make may be minimal in the overall scheme of the business, but they could have a meaningful impact on the bottom line.

Here are some thoughts on the topic.

There may be ways to tweak your product or service that will entice a new set of customers without having to engage additional human resources, raise additional funding or placing a strain on your cash flow.

Start with your operating costs. First, discard those products not generating a profit. Next, find ways to reduce the costs of materials, transport and packaging but without compromising quality. Are your advertising efforts generating sales or do they need a fresh approach? Tweaking product descriptions can make them more attractive to the consumer; similarly with your landing or sales pages. And don't be afraid to ask your customers what they think.

Are you in a line of business that could benefit from referral arrangements? For example, I know business consultants who have established formal arrangements with the legal fraternity where each refers prospective clients to the other. This kind of innovative thinking generates additional income without incurring costs.

The idea is to get smarter at what you do without incurring too much additional workload or having to lay out large amounts of cash. Using the health care professional scenario - depending on the nature of the treatment or care, it may be possible to run group sessions as opposed to a one-on-one treatment. The customer base is increasing and thereby your turnover but not adding additional hours to your workday.

Be creative!

DESIGNING AN EXIT STRATEGY

You may be wondering why I include a section on getting out of your business after spending so much time talking about how to get it started?

Having an exit strategy, or the way in which you intend to dispose of the company or your ownership in it can be an important question for a potential investor and there is no reason why you shouldn't put some thought to it at this early stage.

It may come down to the very reason you are starting the business. You want to create a family business, and the intention is that you will bow out gracefully after several years and hand over the business to your children.

You may also be starting the business with the intention of ultimately selling it and using the proceeds to launch another venture.
Then, of course, there is the unthinkable prospect of having an exit plan should it become apparent the business is failing.

Although all of this may be way off in the future it is not a bad idea to give the subject some thought if you have not already decided on how you foresee the future.

Here is an article on the website **The Balance Small Business** titled *How to Pick an Exit Strategy for Your Small Business* exploring possible exit strategies.

EMPLOYING STAFF

An almost unavoidable consequence of growing any business is the commensurate increase in personnel.

Bringing total strangers into your home-based business will probably be the single most difficult decision you will have to make in the early stages of your business career. And it is one that should not be taken lightly. Human resources could end up being a major portion of your operating costs, and therefore it is paramount that the cost is offset by a noticeable increase in revenue.

Knowing when to employ staff for your business is a conundrum all of its own. The small business environment differs greatly from the corporate world, and this can make finding the right employee more difficult.

Although I continually refer to "small business owners" in the rest of this section, it includes, by implication, "home business owners" although much of what is discussed applies more to the home-based business that is considering expanding beyond a home-based office.

As any small business owner knows, there is more to having staff than simply sharing out the workload; there needs to be depth in the company, and this need arises from two distinct criteria.

The first is that the company needs to operate even when you are not around. Continuity in your absence, whether forced or voluntary, is a key to long-term survival.

The second is the good warm feeling that your big company customers must have that there is more to your company than just you. They need to know that they are dealing with an entity and not an individual.

But of course, you first need to find the right folks that not only will meet the performance requirements of their job but will also acclimatize to the small business environment which can be a culture shock if their background is in corporates or large companies.

Finding someone who not only fits the job description but is prepared to sign up for the long haul can be very difficult. The experts tell us that a staff turnover of under 15% shows a healthy environment, but let's be honest, even the happiest of employees will move on, eventually.

Let's be frank. Smaller companies are generally unable to compete either on salary or more importantly with company benefits with their larger counterparts. Offering staff employment benefits such as a pension scheme, medical insurance or unemployment insurance is sometimes beyond the financial capability of a small business.

My experience has shown that folks who are attracted to the larger business entities tend to stay in that employment circle. Rarely will a 20-year veteran of corporate employment make the crossover to a small company. Their experience and salary threshold are usually an immediate barrier for the small business owner. They are just too experienced and skilled to be attracted to the challenges of small business.

Does this mean the small business owner should be looking for a different kind of employee one that is more suited to the way small businesses operate? And if so, are these employees difficult to find?

As I understand it, the attributes a small business owner would look for in a potential employee don't differ greatly from those sought after by larger companies. But is there something different about a small business employee?

There are only 3 things I can identify.

- They are happy to work on their own [and are not necessarily team players]. This may stem from a social outlook—they don't like crowds or feel uncomfortable being assessed by coworkers.

- They may also prefer self-measurement—they want to be judged on their own performance and not that of the collective. They will have growth aspirations, but it may be more about learning a cross section of responsibilities as opposed to specializing.

- They may have an interest in owning their own small business one day. What better way to learn how to run a small business than working for one?

Let's assume you employ the right individual for your small company. How do you keep them? You probably don't have a suitable range of benefits to offer and the salary scale is perhaps lower than that offered by the big guys—so what do you do?

- Create a growth path for key employees—this is discussed in the Human Resources Plan below.

- Communicate with employees—no-one likes to be kept in the dark. Be prepared to share the goals and aims of the company and inform staff of both the ups and the downs of the business. Something I found seriously lacking in the corporate world.

- Design an incentive scheme but be careful. Increases or bonuses and even the odd paid day off are not a guarantee of contented employees. Many studies have shown that being involved, respected for their skills and knowledge and acknowledged for their contributions are often rated higher by employees than money.

- Develop a "family" environment. This means getting to know your employees, what they are about, their personal goals and what drives them.

- Try the "team" approach. I know small business owners who have been very successful in this area by focusing on team building even outside the work environment. For example, they have a company soccer team that takes part in in-door soccer tournaments. But if one or more employees shy away from this form of group activity, don't pressure them, find other ways to incorporate them into the "family".

- Invest in a balanced work/lifestyle approach. Make sure employees take their annual leave when it is due. Be cognizant of their family requirements and support them where necessary.

- Involve employees. Keep everyone in the loop. Ask for input and don't be afraid to implement and reward good ideas.

- Encourage learning. Support employees who are studying to better themselves even if it is only to give them paid time off to write their examinations.

- As soon as the company can afford to offer employees the traditional company benefits such as a pension scheme, medical insurance, do so.

- Cross train wherever possible. Multi-skilled employees often feel more empowered and satisfied with their personal development.

Much of the above should be applied to all employees irrespective of the size of the company they work for but small business owners have a unique opportunity to get to know their employees really well, simply because there are fewer of them.

Have a Human Resources plan

Your staff recruitment plan should be aligned with your business growth plan. If you intend to increase your sales, then have a plan for creating a structured sales department—don't employ haphazardly. If you need temporary relief to clear a logjam, then employ temporary staff.

Don't be afraid to allocate extra responsibilities and accountabilities to employees. Those who react well to the added pressure could be your future management team. But remember the old adage: good sales people don't necessarily make good sales managers.

Employ wisely and selectively from the beginning.

Virtual and temporary employees

It is becoming common practice for home and small business owners to outsource portions of their workload to external service providers. Your accountant visits your offices once a month to update your books or your marketing strategy is being compiled by an expert in another city or even another country and you correspond by email and Skype.

The reasons for opting for this form of support could be varied, but the most common are:

- they tend to be cheaper than using permanent staff;

- the requirement is of short duration, and

- some home businesses do not have the floor space to accommodate permanent employees, or don't feel comfortable with strangers working in their homes.

Bringing strangers into your home

Which brings us to the tricky problem of home-business owners bringing new people into their inner sanctuary. If you do elect to employ permanent staff there are several issues to keep in mind.

- Unlike larger companies, space is a problem. They need to have their own "work center" and unless you have built a dedicated office in your backyard, you will be bumping into one another, so choose wisely when employing.

- They will have access to your home which could create further pressure on your partner and/or stay at home children.

- Rules need to be set down and communicated. For example; the on-suite bathroom should be off limits as should children's bedrooms and play areas. If they have use of the kitchen area, a "clean up after yourself" rule must be implemented.

- While being careful not to discriminate, if you are a family of non-smokers, employing someone who smokes may be a habit that is just not acceptable in your home.

Labor law requirements

Be sure to seek professional advice before you employ staff, especially permanent staff. Be familiar with the labor laws applicable in your country and employment contracts will have to be drafted and signed by all employees. You will need to draft a Job Description detailing the responsibilities and accountabilities applicable for the position you intend to fill.

This may sound obvious but please ensure that your financial position is secure for the medium to long term. There is nothing more destructive to both yourself and an employee than having to lay someone off prematurely because you didn't do your sums correctly.

Step 5 – The Financial Plan

Note: any references to "small businesses" in this chapter includes home-based businesses.

As you have already read, I believe businesses go under because they run out of money. When starting out as a new entrepreneur, you must ensure your new venture is not constrained by a cash flow problem from the beginning. Making sure you have enough liquidity to maintain the business through its growing pains until it at least breaks even, in addition to meeting the monthly personal expenses, is an absolute MUST.

Accomplishing this may mean cutting back on some of those "nice to have's" like the best computer available or a company car, and allocating your money wisely, keeping the wolves from the door while at the same time funding your launch. Not an easy task.

Be prudent—think BIG but start SMALL. Size your operation in accordance with your budget and stick to your budget. The fancy things can come later when your company is rocketing along, and growth is just the natural next step.

Let's break down the various aspects of your "Financial Plan" and I would suggest using a spreadsheet of sorts, or as I like to do in the initial stages, a great big whiteboard.

If you have not yet decided on what it is the business will offer, this exercise may appear to be haphazard, but I would guess that your short list will provide you with some indication of what the business will look like, so no effort will be wasted.

Your goal is to get a good gut feel as to what your financial needs, or predicament, is likely to be.

Your financial model will consist of 4 elements. These are:

- your personal financial status;

- what funds you have allocated to the business or to supplement your personal shortfall [savings];

- the anticipated start-up costs for the business, and;

- the anticipated operating costs for the business, including all the financially related issues you highlighted in the previous 4 planning steps.

ITEMIZING YOUR FINANCIAL PLAN

It is now time to itemize and document each element of your business that will accrue expenditure.

Your personal financial status

Before you begin this exercise, allow me to share an opinion that I believe should not be negotiable -

Do not include in any business-related calculations finances that are set aside for insurance policies, education, or emergency needs. This is your lifeline and must not be tampered with. If you do not have sufficient funds for the business, give serious consideration to remaining in your permanent employment until you have built up an ADDITIONAL nest egg.

The natural tendency when starting a new venture is to do the math in such a way as to substantiate the viability of the undertaking. This can take the form of sacrifices being made on a personal level to ensure that there is enough money to make the business survive the first dreaded 12 months.

Although admirable, these financial sacrifices often pressure the business owner, and more adversely, their loved ones.

We have all, at one time or another, heard, read or even witnessed, tragic stories of individuals and families whose lives have been devastated when that "sure-fire" opportunity goes south, leaving nothing but financial ruin and human suffering. In most cases, this has been brought about by bad money management.

Make sure you keep the home fires burning before lighting new bush fires for the business.

Whether you are single or married with, or without a family, you need to determine whether your monthly income, after you launch the business, will exceed or at least match your monthly expenses.

This refers to monies that will come into the household, but excluding your expected income from sales from the business. What you are doing here is to assess what income will be available to cover monthly living expenses which would include mortgage or rent payments, living expenses, education fees and other personal or family-related costs. This has nothing to do with the running of the business; it's what you need to survive until such time as the business turns a profit.

If you will no longer be employed, the monthly income may comprise your partner's salary and other extraneous sources such as rent from a property you own, royalties, pension payments, etc.

Keep in mind that the duration of this "survival mode" depends on how soon your business turns a profit.

If your expenses will exceed your monthly personal income, it means you will need to dip into some form of savings to keep yourself, and loved ones, from starvation. Hence my insistence on ensuring your piggy bank caters for more than just the needs of the business.

Company expenses

The first step is to ascertain what money you will need for both the start-up and for a period of trading. Let's start at the beginning.

In Part 1, we looked at the formation of the company and what it required for the first day of operating, what you needed to kick-start the business. We now need to calculate what the **cost of starting the company** will be, in other words, your start-up commitment.

This would include any specialized equipment to make the product or to provide a service as well as office equipment including computers, telephone connection, furniture, etc. You will also need to calculate the cost of the first batch of stationery, including brochures, flyers, and business cards. If you are using a website, the set-up costs are part of the start-up expenses. Don't ignore the low-cost items; lots of small costs can add up to a big headache if not accounted for. This paragraph refers to those items that you will purchase outright. We will cover leases, rental hire purchase agreements later. Don't forget to include the company registration fees and any external consultant charges related to the start-up.

Step 2 is to decide if you will draw a **monthly salary** and if so, how much?

Monthly operating costs such as stationery, utility costs, website fees, and internet connectivity charges, telephone bills, and other costs that the business will incur each month, irrespective of the number of products or services sold, needs to be calculated.

Any monthly repayment obligations. We will discuss borrowing money for the business in some detail below, but if you have already committed to a loan, you will need to record the monthly repayment amount. This also applies to any equipment you acquired through a lease or hire purchase agreements—total up all the monthly payment obligations you will incur.

Go back to your **marketing and growth plan**s and check on what costs you allocated when you compiled those plans. Add them to your cost sheet.

The first production run. If you are providing a service or selling eBooks for example through a website, then this paragraph is not relevant. However, I would point out that if you are selling items such as eBooks, paintings, drawings, and recipes or similar such commodities through a website you need to ensure that you have a reasonable selection available on day one to entice customers.

If you are selling a tangible product, like our favorite cupcakes, you will need to calculate the total cost of your first and subsequent batches that will comprise your first offerings to the market place [keep storage in mind]. Use the numbers you calculated in step 2— **The Product**.

This can be a chicken and egg situation—if you sell nothing for the first 3 months you will only have the cost of one batch, however, if you sell in month one you must ensure that you plow back all the proceeds into making more product.

Let's summarize our cost sheet.

Start-up—a once off cost

And then separately, the monthly costs for:

- salary
- operations
- repayments
- Marketing
- Growth
- first production run

Total up the monthly column.

So, now you have a fair idea of what it will cost to start the business and what the first month of running costs will be.

The next step is to decide when you believe you will sell your first product and how many. Difficult? Absolutely, but you need to make an educated guess because you need to know how long you need to carry the business until the breakeven point is reached.

Once you decide on a period, let's assume it is 2 months, add another 3 months and use this as your **no profit zone**—assume the worst in that you will make no sales in this period.

Multiply the number of months by the monthly cost aggregate. This, together with your start-up total, is the finances you will need in the worst-case scenario, in this example; no sales for the first 5 months.

Your first priority is to ensure that you can cover all your personal and household obligations with your monthly income, now that you will no longer be bringing home a regular salary. The surplus will go into your personal savings I hope.

The second priority is to ascertain whether you have the requisite funds to finance the start-up cost and meet the monthly running costs until monthly business income equals monthly business expenses, or at least covers the "no profit" period

This quick calculation should give you a clear picture whether, financially, you are in a sound position to start a business without incurring risk or placing the family in a precarious position.

If you feel confident enough in the eventual success of your business idea, it may encourage you to look for additional funding should your initial calculations reflect a shortfall, for either monthly needs or start-up requirements. The main consideration when thinking about external funding is that it will need to be repaid, usually with interest over a fixed period.

These repayments must be factored into your monthly expenses for the business. If you are not comfortable with how this should be done, find an accountant. It is imperative that these repayment calculations are accurate.

FINANCING OPTIONS

When first sitting down to assess your financial situation the initial question that you need to answer is simple, do you have a pot of gold under your bed available to invest without placing a financial strain on your day-to-day living expenses and/or for emergencies?

If the answer is "yes" then financially, you are good to go, you just need to detail your plan on how you intend to spend it, all of which is explained below.

If the answer is "no" then you need to look more closely at what will be required to fund the start-up and the operating costs of the proposed business going forward. If there will be a need to provide additional funds to get the business going you need to put some thought to how you will raise these funds and the various options available to you are discussed in this section. Should the thought of how you will go about financing your venture scares the living crap out of you don't be embarrassed to seek professional help and guidance from reputable consultants or financial institutions.

But before you go spending your hard-earned pennies with someone else let's explore the basics of financing a business in layman's terms.

The need for financing usually arises from one of 4 scenarios:

- you need to purchase specialized equipment for the business, i.e. start-up costs;

- there are insufficient funds to cover the anticipated personal and business needs including start-up costs and the period before breakeven is reached;

- although able to fund the start-up costs and the monthly personal needs, the raw material requirements for the first several months will not be covered by your existing savings or personal monthly income;

- or combinations of the above.

There are several ways to raise additional finance for your business, some less risky than others.

But because new small business start-ups lack a trading history, financial credibility, and limited assets which could be considered as collateral for a loan, raising external finance may be difficult.

Option 1—Own resources

The first option is to fund the entire operation from your own resources. This will leave you obligation free from external creditors but may place a strain on your own personal situation. If you can afford to use this option, without jeopardizing the financial wellbeing of your family and being able to fund all the needs of the new business for at least 4—6 months [or until breakeven is reached], it is the best route to go.

Self-funding is perhaps the most common method used by new online start-ups, although not exclusively. There is no reason a "brick and mortar" business cannot also use this approach. The concept is to start the business with minimal expenses and then reinvest all profits into growing the business. Known as "bootstrapping" or "plow back", this method places the least strain on the personal finances and requires very little need to raise external funding for the start-up or operating expenses. The downside is that until the business turns a reasonable profit, which can be plowed back into growth, it remains stagnant.

Option 2—borrow from friends and family

The next option is to borrow from family or friends. Looking back over the years and the various start-up clients I have worked with, this is one of the preferred methods for home-based businesses excluding online launches. The vast majority of my clients have used funds obtained from family and occasionally from friends.

One observation I would make is that when the businesses are successful, there have been minimal problems and the money has been paid back as agreed. However, sometimes where things have gone sour, the resulting fallout has been devastating to all concerned. I have a personal rule: I do not mix financial business arrangements with family or friends, but each to their own. Do not rely on "handshake" arrangements. Get a professional to draft a legally binding agreement between all the parties involved.

Option 3—Public or Private Sector Support

Getting support from government, non-Governmental Organizations [NGOs] or the private sector.

In some countries, there are specific small business programs that are launched and managed by government departments, NGOs and in some cases even private sector companies. The aim of these programs is to stimulate the small business sector and thereby the economy as a whole, with substantial emphasis on disadvantaged communities.

One way to find out if these stimulus packages exist is to contact the relevant government departments direct or approach your local bank and enquire—they should be able to provide a list of what is available. Your Chamber of Commerce is another potential source for information.

The packages often come with stringent rules and regulations and sometimes require that the business is comanaged by the benefactor for a defined period after start-up. Depending on the support provided, the funds loaned to the business are either written off by the lending institution once the company moves into profit or are paid back, interest-free, after an unusually long grace period.

Option 4 - Financial lending institutions.

This would include banks, Finance Houses and the like. If you have ever applied for a personal loan from your bank, you will have some idea what borrowing from these folks is all about.

My advice? If you intend to go this route, you will need a FORMAL Business Plan [BP] and it would be best to hire a professional to compile the document for you. This professional should not only be able to compile the BP for you but must have a proven financial background. There is no point in having a stunning looking BP only to have it ripped apart because the financials are incorrect or incomplete.

Option 5—Other financial sources

Angel Investors

If you have not heard of these individuals or organizations this explains who they are and what they provide.

"Definition: An individual who invests his or her own money in an entrepreneurial company.

Originally a term used to describe investors in Broadway shows, 'angel' now refers to anyone who invests his or her money in an entrepreneurial company [unlike institutional venture capitalists, who invest other people's money]. Angel investing has soared in recent years as a growing number of individuals seek better returns on their money than they can get from traditional investment vehicles. Contrary to popular belief, most angels are not millionaires. Typically, they earn between $60,000 and $100,000 a year. Which means there are likely to be plenty of them right in your own backyard.

Angels come in two varieties: those you know and those you don't know. They may include professionals such as doctors and lawyers; business associates such as executives, suppliers and customers; and even other entrepreneurs. Unlike venture capitalists and bankers, many angels are not motivated solely by profit. Particularly if your angel is a current or former entrepreneur, he or she may be motivated as much by the enjoyment of helping a young business succeed as by the money he or she stands to gain. Angels are more likely than venture capitalists to be persuaded by an entrepreneur's drive to succeed, persistence and mental discipline.

Angel investors vary widely, but they are typically willing to accept risk and demand little or no control in return for the chance to own a piece of a business that may be valuable someday."

Extract from an article *Angel Investor - Small Business Encyclopedia,* on **Entrepreneur.com**

In an article on the Forbes website titled: *What small business owners should know about Angel Investors,* the author has the following to say:

"What are the six most important things for angel investors?

Here are what angels particularly care about:

- *The quality, passion, commitment, and integrity of the founders.*
- *The market opportunity being addressed and the potential for the company to become very big.*
- *A clearly thought out business plan, and any early evidence of obtaining traction toward the plan.*
- *Interesting technology or intellectual property.*
- *An appropriate valuation with reasonable terms.*
- *The viability of raising additional rounds of financing if progress is made."*

Crowd funding.

This is a method whereby you ask a group of total strangers to assist the launch of your business, or development of your product or idea, by donating small amounts of cash to you in exchange for a gift.

The advantage is that the donors have no recourse to you or the business; they don't get shares [unless you offer them in exchange for substantial donations], they have no say in the running of the business, and once you deliver your gift to them, the transaction, and therefore the obligations, are fulfilled on both sides.

The downside is that the sites on which this is transacted are busy, so you will compete against thousands of other fundraisers.

In brief, this is how it works.

You need money to launch your business or a product—this could be in concept or idea stage to begin with.

You join one or more of the sites online and you enter all the information requested by the site. This describes what you want the money for, a sales pitch about the business or product which will include video [by you] and relevant images.

You declare how much you want, and you then set cash donation categories against which you offer a gift. To illustrate: you accept donations of $1, $5, $10, $25 and $50. For $1, you will thank the donor but for $50 you will send them a free product [you can limit the number of gifts at the higher levels, say a free product for the first 100 donations of $50].

You set a cut-off date and then you wait. Some sites will give you what money comes in, but others will return the money to the donors if you do not meet the target.

This process of raising funds was made famous by sites such as **Kickstarter** and **Indiegogo** amongst others. I have used Crowd Funding to finance product development and was successful with 2 and not so lucky with 1. My opinion is that they favor product funding as opposed to start-up funding for a home business. Assuming I am correct it would be better to pitch for the product you want to make rather than trying to raise funds to operate your business.

There is an article on **The Balance Small Business** titled *The 7 Best Crowdfunding Sites of 2019* that offer to fund small business start-ups and appear to operate similarly to those mentioned above. I have only used 2 of them, so I cannot offer an opinion on the suitability of the others

Summary

Remember, the less risk you can start your business with, the better. Having a repayable loan hanging over your head from day one is something best avoided if possible. Being in debt from the outset can be a heavy burden to carry along with all the other stresses and worries you will inherit as an entrepreneur.

I know it is very tempting to cut loose and go on your own but be "penny wise and pound wise". Being able to say "I have my own business" may be a great ego booster over a few drinks with friends, but conversely, it will be ego destroying when you have to admit six months later that you are looking for a job because you didn't plan your finances.

MANAGING YOUR FINANCES

Cash flow is King [or Queen—whichever you prefer] is a statement you will encounter over and over as you delve more deeply into the "how's" of owning a new business.

The fact is, it is true. Unless you have more pennies in your account, or at least due to you, than you have to pay out each month, your business is going to crash!

Not a good place to be.

To avoid this unpleasant situation, you need to have more than just a finger on the pulse of your business daily; you need to have your whole hand monitoring every transaction, especially in the beginning. And by beginning, I mean the first 18-24 months, at least—thereafter you will be able to afford to use a full-time accountant to manage it for you.

Here are some tips on managing your finances on a day-to-day basis:

Credit cards

My suggestion? Stay away from them until your business is settled and turning a profit. Rather use a debit or cash card for those everyday consumables spends. This will make sure you only spend what you have. When purchasing raw materials or components for your product, it is preferable to have an arrangement with your suppliers that allows you to pay by Electronic Funds Transfer or EFT. It is cheaper and just as reliable. Try and stay away from any payment system that will incur indirect costs, such as interest.

Terms of Payment

There are 2 aspects to payment terms.

The first—is the terms of payment you will impose on your customers. If at all possible, there should be only one choice. Payment against delivery. If you are selling very high-priced commodities that undergo a manufacturing period, try to negotiate extended payment terms. This means that a form of "deposit" is paid over before the manufacturing cycle begins and thereafter part payments are made during and on completion of manufacture.

For example, you make electric gates, which require the purchase of materials that have an extended lead-time and then you still need to manufacture the gate. Your payment terms could be; 25% with order, 50% midway through manufacture and 25% on delivery. This assists with the upfront purchase of the materials you need and ensures a commitment from the buyer and provides a leverage should the buyer become "difficult" during the process.

Some small manufacturers require the customer to pay the portion that makes up the material cost at the time of order. If the materials you need to make a gate will cost you 40% of your total cost [not your selling price] then you would insist on an equivalent payment with order.

As you develop your relationships with your repeat customers, they may approach you for preferential payment terms. This will need to be negotiated and whether you should offer payment discounts [e.g. 30 days less 2.5%] is a financial decision that you should discuss with your accountant.

My advice to all small business owners is that wherever possible, stick with Cash against Delivery payment terms unless the nature or price of your product dictates otherwise.

The second aspect is the terms of payment imposed on you as a buyer of materials, components, office consumables, etc.

In the real world, you will encounter difficulties with this one. Suppliers demand cash on delivery with all new small businesses until a proven payment track record is established.

There is not a lot that can be done to counter this, other than trying to negotiate more favorable terms with the supplier as your relationship develops. Some small business owners offer to forego volume discounts for longer payment terms, but you need to do the math to see if this is viable.

The whole idea behind managing payment terms, both inward and outward, is to maintain a positive cash flow.

Large orders

There will come a time when you are confronted with a customer who is so enamored with your product they place a high volume order.

This can be a problem if you need to purchase raw materials for manufacture to meet the order, in other words, you may need to lay out a large payment before you can even begin the work.

There are, however, some very real positives to taking on your first large order.

- You will be in a better position to negotiate a discount on the increased raw material purchase.

- Your company profile will be enhanced amongst the buying community.

- It could be the first step in your growth plan.

There are two ways in which you can accommodate the added expense of fulfilling the order.

- Negotiate an up-front payment that will fund the purchase of the raw materials. You may need to offer a discount on the selling price as an incentive for the buyer to part with their money in advance.

- Approach your bank for a short-term loan that will cover the raw material purchase. This will depend on your relationship with the bank manager, but funding institutions are more amenable to providing help where there is proof of eventual payment which will more than cover the loan.

If your business is a new customer with the bank, you may be asked to agree to what is called "factoring" the order in my part of the world. In simple terms, what this means is that the bank may insist that the buyer makes all payments, regarding the order, to them as opposed to you. This gives the bank a good warm feeling in their water that they will get their money back. Once the order is delivered and paid for, the bank will deduct their loan, plus interest, and pay the rest to you. This method can also be a nice way to establish a working relationship with the bank. By the same token, some customers find this "financial management arrangement" very acceptable and the reason is that they believe the "deal" is a lot more credible when a bank is involved.

Swapping or "bartering"

I include this only because I have often been asked about the feasibility of these types of arrangements. Although there is money to be saved, the problem with exchanging goods or services with another company is the practicality of implementation.

In essence, what happens is you may offer your services or products in exchange for a service or product from another home or small business and there is no exchange of money. For example, you may offer your accounting services in exchange for a monthly supply of printer cartridges.

The problem comes about when both parties assess the value of what they get for what they give away. This is often difficult to equate and can lead to recriminations.

It can, however, be an option on a "once-off" basis. I will do your year-end financial statements for you re-wiring the electrics in my office—as an example.

Monitoring casual expenditure

It is amazing how much "small change" gets spent by small and home business owners, particularly in the early months of operation. Lunches, snacks, nice to have office gadgets, drinks with potential customers, and so the list goes on. While some of these expenses could bring in new business, often they are unnecessary but can have a serious impact on your cash flow over time if not monitored.

Keep all receipts and invoices and make the time to assess the damage at the end of each month. Determine what adds value to the business and what is wastage.

Keep business and family expenses separate and don't get into the habit of cross payments using the family credit card to purchase items for the business and vice versa. Over time, you will assess where private expenditure can be written off to the business, such as part of your mortgage or rent payments, but in the beginning, keep them separate.

Budget controls

We will get into your budget in the next section but suffice to say at this stage—manage your budget carefully. Don't commit to spending what you don't or will not have come payment time.

Keep that cash flow POSITIVE at all times!

The "Shiny New Toys," syndrome

This malignant mental disorder is a disease often experienced by new entrants to certain professions, such as starting a new business. It rears its ugly head in the form of tantalizing new sources of enlightenment that are skillfully laid before the unsuspecting learner. The new entrepreneur, believing that they need to determine "how to be a successful business owner in 3 easy steps" as fast as possible, spend copious amounts of money on dubious courses, eBooks, videos and other online goodies.

As each shiny new toy is purchased, a new and even more exciting find is uncovered (known as sales funnels), and so the quest continues, and equally so, the bank balance diminishes.

Don't get me wrong, there is a multitude of great books and courses available online that are value for money, conversely, there are a bunch of scams and unfortunately, it is not too difficult to get caught up in the knowledge hype. I was temporarily inflicted with this malady until cured by several slaps to the head by my accountant and a severe rebuke from my bank manager.

There is nothing wrong with paying for knowledge or expertize as and when you believe there is no other way of attaining the information. But, [here he goes again] pinpoint what it is you need to learn, research the opportunities available [preferably the free ones], ask around from trusted sources and then spend your money wisely.

You will be pleasantly surprised what you will find in your local library [yes, the big brick building I referred to previously] and through learning institutions such as universities and colleges. There are massive amounts of free knowledge available online from very reputable sites and authors, my learning of how to build a WordPress site is an example.

I have always been an ardent reader and although a useful source, my most valued sources for business-related information is other small business owners and my mentors. Remember, unlike the theorists, they have been there, done it [both successfully and unsuccessfully] and own multiple T-shirts verifying their experiences.

MONITORING YOUR CASH FLOW AND STARTING A BUDGET

The purpose of documenting your financial transactions is to provide you with a visual tool that will allow you to keep track of your sales, and the resultant income, and all your outgoing expenditures in the form of supplier payments for raw materials, consumables and other expenses the business will incur.

What is required is that you get into the habit of keeping close tabs on what you are doing financially in the business. There are various ways to keep track of these transactions.

Here are 3 options in addressing your financial and accounting needs:

- you can do the accounting yourself with packages such as Quickbooks, but this requires some basic understanding of accounting fundamentals and undergoing training;
- you could appoint a full-time accountant should your financial reserves allow for it, or
- do as many new home and micro start-ups do, do it yourself and when funds permit, use a part-time accountant, one day a month, getting your books up to date.

I used Excel spreadsheets to keep a record of all incomes and payments, cash flow, and sales projections.

My accountant had access to these files and together with the hard copy documents, she could annotate my accounting records in her system each month. It makes the annual returns easy to compile, and she is confident in their accuracy when submitting the final tax return.

If MS Office is a bit out of your price range or you just don't like Excel here are other FREE options [at the time of writing] for spreadsheet-based programs:

Google Sheets

Apache Open Office [for Windows, Mac, and Linux]

Zoho Sheet [free and paid versions]

LibreOffice

I have used none of them, so I am not in a position to comment on their suitability, however from what I read in terms of product reviews, they all appear to do the job.

Isn't this duplication? Yes, it is but the reason I used this system in my early entrepreneurial days was that I had a real-time visual understanding of my projections versus actual expenditures. All the spreadsheets were interlinked so an additional transaction in one account rolls through several summaries and ends up updating my cash flow and projection statements. I don't have to keep calling my accountant every time I need to know what I have spent or committed to for the future.

When you start out, it may appear to be overkill to be spending time and money on creating detailed accounts when your incomes and expenditures are limited to a handful of activities and only occur during the last few days of each month. And you would be correct. However, if you intend to grow your business, now is the time to develop the insight and skills required to design and manage your budget, be it both for financial reasons and forecasting purposes.

After year one it is time to start developing a forecast budget. This is the forecast of projected income and expenditure for the following 12 or more months.

One of the building blocks for your financial budget is the recording of individual transaction records [accounts] for all your activities, whether it be sales through your website, paying suppliers for raw materials needed to make your product or the money spent on that lunch with a prospective customer.

How you design this system is up to you, but I would recommend that you avoid hoarding invoices, payment records and till slips in places like shoeboxes. Establish a system that is both visual and easily interrogated, making things easy to find when you need them. This could be done with an accounting package and all hard copy documents logically filed and stored in an area that is accessible and out of the way of natural mishaps like a leaking roof.

Set aside a fixed period for updating your financial records. It may only be an hour once a week when you first start out but could become more as your business grows, but whatever it is, stick to the routine.

YEAR-END FINANCIAL STATEMENTS

If you still need a good reason to get bogged down with all this apparent paperwork, then think no further than your friendly taxman.

Unless your company structure excludes the need to submit annual financial returns to the government, you will have to comply with this regulation, willingly or otherwise. Keeping your financial transactions up to date, accurate, and with easy access to all the supporting documentation will make compiling your returns that much quicker and simpler. Even more so if you get audited with little prior notice.

The registration of a legal entity, such as a company, is governed by legislation, sometimes known as the "Company's Act" or something similar. The Act describes all the requirements, obligations and responsibilities associated with owning and running a company, irrespective of its nature.

Part of this will be the requirements to keep records, as they pertain to Company Taxation. The Act will specify how tax returns should be submitted and when, how records must be kept [digital or hard copy], for how long and whether they are to be audited by an external body or whether the owner may submit the annual returns.

Therefore, accurate record keeping is a good habit to develop from the very outset of your business. Discuss the requirements with your accountant, particularly if he or she will prepare monthly accounts for you besides compiling your annual tax return.

If you intend to do it yourself, familiarize yourself with the Act, then design a system that not only complies with the legislation but is practical and makes document recovery easy. You don't want to be panicking because you can't find that shoebox with all your receipts in when you are audited.

As a business owner, you will be required to keep records of all orders [incoming and outgoing], invoices, receipts, proof of payments, bank statements, contracts, letters of appointment, staff payment and deduction records and any other transactional documents related to the business. Also, remember to keep a record of tax submissions together with all supporting documentation. Depending on what deductions you are allowed for having a home-based business, you may also need to keep proof of payments for rent, mortgage, insurance, and utilities. And keep your company registration papers in a very safe place.

If you are permitted to have digital files, then you need to create backups of your records. I keep a full back up on my PC, one on an external hard drive and another on an external or *cloud* site, such as One Drive, Google Drive, or DropBox.

The relevant Act will also tell how long you are required to hold a document in storage. In my part of the world, most documents must be kept for 3 years after which they can be destroyed. You are unlikely to be drawn and quartered if you hold them for longer. I keep copies of personal and company tax returns forever.

FINANCIAL RECORD KEEPING

Maintaining accurate and up to date financial records can be a time-consuming exercise, especially in the beginning but as your business progresses and you become more acquainted with what financial information you need, it will get more streamlined.

To help, the following is one option for capturing and maintaining your financial information. It is not the only way and as I mentioned; you need to find what works for you. Talk to your accountant, mentor or friends, and family members who either have accounting experience or more appropriately, own a home or small business.

For this walkthrough, I am assuming you have elected to use a spreadsheet program of some sort.

Gathering and collating information

As you go through the preparation or start-up phase for the business, there will be both legal and financial documentation that must be filed away in a safe place as already mentioned. These could include the company registration papers, bank account details, Tax submission requirements, employee contracts, rental or lease agreements, loan agreements, and insurance policies. Make scanned, digital copies of these documents and file them in different places as suggested above.

It is also possible that you have made purchases for the start-up. This may include specialized equipment, computer or office furniture. You must keep all the documents related to the purchases and ensure they are filed with all other start-up related information. You will need them for your first-year tax returns.

As the business begins to operate, you will place orders for your raw materials [or go to the supplier and buy them over the counter] for which payments will need to be made. Likewise, you will purchase consumables and stationery for your office, possibly a whiteboard, computer accessories and so on.

This means order forms [if you have negotiated delayed payment terms with suppliers], invoices, till receipts, delivery notes when the materials are delivered and debit or credit card receipts. If you sell online, the software program you use will generate orders and invoices for each purchase and you need to keep a record of them. Check with the software providers what records are produced and what you need to download and store.

These must be kept, even for the smallest amounts, and filed in a logical order. You may file the document away as soon as you receive it or do so at a later stage, maybe every Friday afternoon is dedicated to admin duties. If so, you will need a method to keep all these documents in a safe place but also which allows for easy filing and retrieval.

Design a filing system that best suits your business. However, be realistic, you need not open a file for the $2 rubber bands you bought, but you may require a file that is marked "Office Stationery" and includes all the receipts for all the different office consumables and stationery purchased each month.

I find it best to start with your highest spend suppliers, for example, if you are going to make and sell cakes you will probably be buying your ingredients from the same supplier or group of suppliers, so you will want to have a file for each supplier.

Group small ad hoc purchases together wherever you can, as explained with the office stationery. If you will be out and about visiting customers or attending product shows or industry seminars, then you may need a file headed "Travel". Advertising is another group that would cover newspaper adverts, online marketing expenses, brochure printing, etc. However, if you use a single agent to manage all of this for you, then your file would be in the agent's name.

Design your "paper trail" before you start the business and get your hard copy filing system in place. Decide whether you will create a digital version [on a spreadsheet] which is advisable, and I will explain why in a moment, and build it.

TRACKING YOUR EXPENDITURE AND INCOME

Let's start with creating a single account or spreadsheet.

For this exercise, it will be for the main supplier of your ingredients for your cake baking business. The account for a month could look something like this.

2019	Supplier	ACME Trading			
March	Order No.	Description	Amount	Paid	Ref
6	1234	Flour	123.50	2019/03/06	Cash
9	5678	Oil	89.00	2019/03/09	Cash
15	9123	Condiments	55.00	2019/03/15	Cash
23	1456	Flour	156.80	2019/03/23	EFT AB789
4		TOTAL	424.30		

March	Order No.	Description	Amount	Paid	Ref
2	2067	Sugar	97.15	2019/04/06	Cash
13	9864	Flour	213.45	2019/04/09	EFT AB340
18	3678	Sugar	97.15	2019/04/15	Cash
3		TOTAL	407.75		

Note: If you describe each purchase as "ingredients" then you would need to keep a list of what you purchased and in what quantities elsewhere. You can do this either in the account or on a separate spreadsheet or link the line item in the account to an invoice or receipt number in your hard copy filing system. It is important to keep track of individual items as it will allow you to compare price trends and usages over time.

The account would be much more detailed and therefore more complex. However, the upside is that you can create, for example, a usage spreadsheet for each item, link it back to the supplier account and it will automatically keep a real-time track of your monthly usages. Likewise, of the individual prices.

You will have a similar account for each of your large monthly, repeat expenditures.

For the trivial, but regular expenses such as your office supplies, the account will look something like this;

Account Office Consumables						
2019						
March	Order No.	Description	Supplier	Amount	Paid	Ref
6	1234	Photocopy paper	Jim's Paper	15.17	03/06/2019	Cash
9	5678	Printer ink	Ink Specialists	9.14	03/09/2019	Cash
15	9123	Various items	CNA	11.28	03/15/2019	Cash
23	1456	Whiteboard	Office Experts	156.80	03/23/2019	Cash
	4		TOTAL	193.39		
April						
2	2067	Files	CNA	23.75	04/02/2019	Cash
13	9864	Printer Cartridges	Print Boss	41.00	04/13/2019	Cash
18	3678	Board markers	Write Nicely	10.10	04/18/2019	
	4		TOTAL	74.85		

Sales

Keeping a track of your monthly sales depends very much on the product, and the method you used to sell it. If you are offering digital products from your website, it is likely that you are running a plugin that will record and report on all the transactions as and when they occur. Some plugins allow for the download of the reports in different formats, Excel, PDF, etc.

If you are selling tangible products "over the counter", then it is probable that you are issuing a hard copy receipt for each payment. These need to be filed away and if you are using a spreadsheet to collate the information for each product, you need to capture the total number of sales over a given period. Depending on the volume of sales, it could be daily, weekly or monthly.

Tracking monthly transactions

From the multiple individual accounts, it is now necessary to reflect this information on a single spreadsheet.

This could be in the form of an aggregate of all expense accounts and sales, all rolled up into your monthly income and expenditure statement. This is how I do it:

My "control account" or spreadsheet is two CASH FLOW accounts.

The first is the PROJECTIONS of what is likely to happen for the next 12 months and so this account incorporates financial and sales projections and purchasing activities. What it shows me is:

- ✓ my sales projections for the next 12 months.
- ✓ expected income from the projections.
- ✓ less all costs associated with producing the product.

Which shows projected GROSS PROFIT per month.

- ✓ Less projected Fixed Operating expenses per month.

Which then gives me a projected CASH FLOW status for each month.

	Mo.1	Mo.2	Mo.3	Mo.4	Mo.5	Mo.6	Mo.7	Mo.8	Mo.9	Mo.10	Mo.11	Mo.12
Units sold	3 000	3 000	3 000	3 000	3 000	3 000	3 000	3 000	3 000	3 000	3 000	3 000
Unit price	49.00	49.00	49.00	49.00	49.00	49.00	49.00	49.00	49.00	49.00	49.00	49.00
Unit cost	20.66	20.66	20.66	20.66	20.66	20.66	20.66	20.66	20.66	20.66	20.66	20.66
Price to resellers	23.40	23.40	23.40	23.40	23.40	23.40	23.40	23.40	23.40	23.40	23.40	23.40
Sales to resellers	88 200	88 200	88 200	88 200	88 200	88 200	88 200	88 200	88 200	88 200	88 200	88 200
Cost of Sales	61 980	61 980	61 980	61 980	61 980	61 980	61 980	61 980	61 980	61 980	61 980	61 980
Gross Profit	26 220	26 220	26 220	26 220	26 220	26 220	26 220	26 220	26 220	26 220	26 220	26 220
Operating costs	11 576	11 576	11 427	11 576	11 576	11 427	11 576	11 576	11 427	11 576	11 427	11 576
Payroll Costs	5 128	5 128	5 128	5 128	5 128	5 128	5 128	5 128	5 128	5 128	5 128	5 128
Payroll Taxes & benefits	615	615	615	615	615	615	615	615	615	615	615	615
General Office requisites	149	149	-	149	149	-	149	149	-	149	-	149
Utilities	239	239	239	239	239	239	239	239	239	239	239	239
Communications charges	1538	1538	1538	1538	1538	1538	1538	1538	1538	1538	1538	1538
Advertising	1282	1282	1282	1282	1282	1282	1282	1282	1282	1282	1282	1282
Travel	641	641	641	641	641	641	641	641	641	641	641	641
Rent	1923	1923	1923	1923	1923	1923	1923	1923	1923	1923	1923	1923
Freight of PCB assemblies	-	-	-	-	-	-	-	-	-	-	-	-
Loan Account repayment	5 000	5 000	5 000	5 000	5 000	5 000	5 000	5 000	5 000	5 000	5 000	5 000
Ongoing Development	-	-	-	5 000	5 000	5 000	8 000	4 000	-	8 000	8 000	-
Software	-	-	-	5 000	5 000	5 000	5 000	4 000	-	5 000	5 000	-
Hardware	-	-	-	-	-	-	3 000	-	-	3 000	3 000	-
Total Costs	16 576	16 576	16 427	21 576	21 576	21 427	24 576	20 576	16 427	24 576	24 427	16 576
PROFIT before Tax	9 644	9 644	9 793	4 644	4 644	4 793	1 644	5 644	9 793	1 644	1 793	9 644
Cash Flow cumulative	9 644	19 288	29 081	33 725	38 369	43 163	44 807	50 451	60 244	61 888	63 681	73 325

What this document is also giving you is your annual BUDGET.

This is a guideline only, but it does allow me to "play" the what if scenarios. Can I afford to purchase extra equipment, should I tap back on incidental expenses, etc.?

You can roll your projections out for as long a period as you deem necessary but keep it within the realm of reality. This is a 3-year projection example:

	Year 1	Year 2	Year 3
Recommended Retail price	49,00	53,90	59,29
Price to Distributors	29,40	32,34	35,57
Sales	1 058 400	2 328 480	3 841 992
Cost of Sales	743 760	1 636 272	2 699 849
Number of units sold	36 000	72 000	108 000
GROSS PROFIT	**314 640**	**692 208**	**1 142 143**
Operating costs	205 815	305 146	423 861
Payroll Costs	61 538	67 692	74 462
Payroll Taxes & benefits	7 385	8 123	8 935
General Office requisites	1 194	1 313	1 445
Utilities	3 582	3 940	4 334
Communications charges	18 462	20 308	22 338
Advertising	15 385	16 923	18 615
Travel	7 692	8 462	9 308
Rent	23 077	25 385	27 923
Freight of PCB assemblies	67 500	153 000	256 500
Loan Account repayments	60 000	50 000	
Ongoing Development	43 000	45 365	47 633
Software	34 000	35 870	37 664
Hardware	9 000	9 495	9 970
Total Operating Costs	308 815	400 511	471 494
PROFIT before Tax	**5 825**	**291 697**	**670 649**

I then create an identical layout on another spreadsheet, but this is for ACTUAL transactions. This is the ACTUAL income and expenditure on a monthly basis. It is to this account that all the sales and expense accounts are linked. As I enter the daily transactions into each of these smaller accounts the aggregated balance for the month is transferred to my ACTUAL spreadsheet.

Through the use of split screens, I can compare projections with actuals. You can combine the projections and actuals onto one enormous spreadsheet, but I have found this cumbersome and even more so if you have multiple products. By comparing my actual cash flow situation to my projected, or budgeted cash flow, I can determine the financial position of the company. It also allows me to determine trends over time such as climate influences, vacation season impact and any other external influences likely to affect my sales.

If working with graphs is your thing, then Excel provides the facility to convert the data into representational depictions of all those transactions you wish to monitor.

Is using this method efficient? In the longer term, I would think not, you need to have a professional accounting package, however, as a starting point, it is enough to enable you to get acclimatized to budgeting and financial management.

But whichever route you choose to follow make sure it is practical and gives you the information you need. Use what is comfortable and works for you and your type of business.

Step 6 – An Analysis of the Business

Time for some introspection—of both yourself and the business idea you have developed. The purpose of this exercise is two-fold. If you intend to compile a formal Business Plan, the bank or prospective business partner will look to this section to assess your analysis of the new company and get an idea of what kind of person you are and what you will bring to the business. If you are doing a plan for the business, it will give you an insight as to where you need help and what elements of the business require your immediate attention.

Completing this step will also highlight anything you may have missed regarding the previous 5 steps, so it is a final checklist before you declare your company ready for launch.

Ah yes, the old fashion, but still very pertinent, SWOT analysis.

Under the following 4 headings, list those aspects, traits, characteristics or circumstances that come to mind and where applicable give thought to how you will address them, now or in the future.

At the moment you are the business and the business is you, much of what you list as personal characteristics and traits will apply to the business, but there will be instances where the nature of the business you have chosen may also highlight aspects that will apply whether or not you own it.

The strengths.

Much of what you list in this category are those things that made you choose the business you have. It goes without saying that these are the things you need to get the most mileage from.

Here are some examples of personal strengths that you could bring to the business, and why.

- ✓ You have a vast knowledge and experience with the product.
- ✓ Good with numbers [do your own accounting].
- ✓ Financially astute—maybe you have compiled a very intricate set of budgets to manage your investments and the family financial accounts. This bodes well for managing the business's financial affairs.
- ✓ People person [good for selling].
- ✓ Articulate [good for cold calling or writing great articles on your website].
- ✓ Bit of a perfectionist [consistent high-quality product].
- ✓ Happy to put in the extra hours [will meet deadlines].
- ✓ Family important [mature outlook to the venture and will establish a balanced approach].
- ✓ Well networked [can only be a positive, irrespective of your business].
- ✓ Will take calculated risks [lending institutions often like this characteristic. It means the owner is looking to grow the business but will only take risks after doing the research and consultations].

From the business perspective, some strengths may be that the model you have chosen is already accepted in the market place and therefore the chances of success with entry and sustainability are better than good. Your product may be unique, but you have identified a definite need and your market research has received a very positive response from the market place.

Maybe you have found a cheaper raw material or ingredient that will allow you to undercut the current market prices without compromising quality.

Weaknesses

These could well be the flip side of some of the strengths listed above. It is important to spend time on this category. Knowing what the weaknesses are will allow you to address them and so avoid serious road bumps in your journey. There may often be costs associated with improving on your personal or company weak spots and so make sure they are included in your financial plan.

Let's look at some potential weaknesses.

Bad with numbers? This will mean that you will need more in the way of accounting support than just submitting your annual accounts to an accountant for tax purposes. Managing the finances of the business is critical so if working with numbers, and in particular with financial related numbers, is a foreseen problem then maybe you need to get some training, at least in the basics.

Struggle to deal with people—having to sell something to someone is your worst nightmare. This is an aspect that hopefully flagged itself right at the beginning of your journey and the reason I mention this is that if it is a crippling concern, it could affect the decision as to what type of business you launch. Maybe you are more suited to an online business where people contact is virtual as opposed to face-to-face. If not, hiring sales staff may be the only way to address this problem in the short term.

The people issues will lead to another weakness—little or no network. This means that penetrating the market will be that much more difficult. This demands developing a marketing strategy that recognizes this shortfall.

Maybe you have theoretical knowledge of the product but lack experience with the "technical issues". For example, you may have artwork that you want to offer via a website, but you have no technical expertize when it comes to the creation of the website.

One of the main weaknesses for any home business owner is the lack of resources in the beginning. Unless you have the financial clout to enable you to employ the staff you need to cover all your bases, you will encounter the usual frustrations of having only one pair of hands to do all the work. This reinforces my earlier advice of thinking big but start small.

As with a lack of human resources, you may also have a finite limit to your finances, which could inhibit growth in the medium to long term.

Sound business sense. This may be learned over time but do whatever you can to be sure you have more than just a basic understanding of how a company operates and what makes markets tick. I have seen too many product smart people go under because they did not grasp the fundamentals of business management. As mentioned previously, a great salesperson does not necessarily make a great sales manager.

Listing your weaknesses is a confrontation with yourself and will test your self-confidence if you allow it to. The idea behind this exercise is not to blow your idea out of the water but to help you identify areas where you may need to focus your energies or to seek help. Acknowledging what you can't do is a positive. You cannot expect to be the master of everything and the sooner you earmark those areas where external help is needed, the quicker you will overcome the weaknesses.

Tip: When you draft your list, use 2 columns. In one, list the weakness and in the second the proposed remedy. This will force you to seek a solution sooner rather than later when the weakness leads to a crippling problem.

Opportunities

Here you are looking at ways in which you can turn potential opportunities into profit-making strategies. Here are some thoughts.

Are there other markets you will be able to enter?

Did your pre-launch marketing highlight any new opportunities regarding markets or new customers?

Have you identified a unique way to add value to your product that is not already being offered?

Can you identify new social media outlets that will attract new potential customers?

Is there a need-solution gap in the market place that you could take advantage of?

Are there environmental or political influences that could open up new markets for you?

Challenges or threats

When listing the threats, consider the following:

Strengths of your competitors—how long have they been around, does it appear that there are new entrants on the horizon and do you expect a reaction from competitors when you first enter the market?

Is there a monopoly in the sector you are entering?

Are there environmental or political changes on the horizon that could negatively impact your business?

Will you need to reassess your technology [if relevant]?

Are there any obstacles or hindrances that you may face as a new entrant, for example, it may take time to attract visitors to your website?

After drawing up your SWOT analysis it is time to take advantage of your strengths, plan to overcome your weaknesses and minimize the impact, decide how best to leverage the opportunities to your advantage and prepare to counter the challenges and threats.

In the next part of this book, Part 3, I am going to introduce you to the processes behind finding and working with a mentor.

PART 3 - Step 7 - Finding and working with a mentor

Introduction to Mentoring

As small or home-based business owners, we often find ourselves caught between a rock and a hard place. We know we need help but don't have the time to find it and so we call on the nearest "we can solve all your problems" consulting company and hope, after recovering from paying the bill, that the quick fix solution has resolved our problem and we can get back to our busy days.

But what if there is a longer-term solution that we could consider?

What if you could find someone with a lifetime of business experiences prepared to share this knowledge with you—and not even charge you!

This is what mentoring, and being mentored is all about, and in this Part 3 I will not only introduce you to the concept but also provide you with a step-by-step process which will enable you to source and engage with your very own personal mentor.

This is not just about how to get help to resolve a specific business-related problem or to address a personal failing. It is about how to identify and implement a long-term support mechanism that could be just a phone call away for the rest of your business career.

Much has been written about the benefits of mentoring and how best it should be implemented, usually regarding the in-company development of staff and managers in training. This Part 3 is however aimed at the home and small business owner and how best he, or she, can find the most suitable mentor and how best to benefit from the process.

The process recommended in this book is based on my own experiences as both mentor and mentee. I have also drawn on the experiences of friends and colleagues [with their permission] who, over many years of business ownership have all, at one time or another, relied on external mentors to either grow or rescue their enterprises.

The book is divided into 2 distinct sections:

Part 3.1—will take you through an overview of what traditional mentoring is all about. How it started, who are mentors and where to find them, what they can do for you and your business and how it compares to the more structured form of training provided by consultants and coaches. A must read if the concept of being mentored is new to you.

Part 3.2—is a guideline for how you, the home or small business owner, can go about finding your very own mentor. It will discuss identifying why you need a mentor, how to find the right one for you, getting prepared for your first meeting, what is required during the mentoring process and finally how the relationship is amicably ended. If you are *au fait* with what mentoring is all about, you may wish to jump to Part 3.2.

Part 3.1 - What Is Mentoring?

"a mentor is someone whose hindsight can become your foresight"
- Author unknown

Some Background

Although there is a plethora of definitions, buzz words and "how to's", being mentored is, in simplistic terms, about getting help from someone more experienced and knowledgeable than yourself.

The **mentor** [that's the guru who has all the answers] is there to provide guidance and help based upon their own extensive knowledge and experience in a given sphere of personal or business development.

The **mentee** also referred to as the protégé [that's you], is there to suck it all up and apply what you learn in an effort to improve your business.

For the purest here are several definitions of mentoring that explain the logic and intent of mentoring or being mentored.

Audrey J. Murrell, Ph.D. [Katz School of Business] in an article titled *Five Key Steps for Effective Mentoring Relationships* states: "Mentoring is not about finding a perfect match or even a single relationship. A more useful definition of mentoring is a collaborative relationship between two or more individuals that supports the career and/or personal development throughout one's career."

The author says:

"This definition is important for several reasons. First, it reminds us that mentoring is about a relationship—it is both dynamic and reciprocal. In effective mentoring relationships, there is an exchange, and both the mentor and the protégé benefit. Relationships are also dynamic which means that mentoring must and will change over time. A focus on the "relationship" aspect of this definition reminds us that mentoring must be cultivated, and requires active participation of both the mentor and the protégé. The third part of this definition directs our attention to the need for developing more than one relationship. Mentoring that helps to support your career requires not just a single mentor but also a network of mentoring relationships."

From Eric Parsloe, The Oxford School of Coaching & Mentoring - "Mentoring is to support and encourage people to manage their own learning in order that they may maximize their potential, develop their skills, improve their performance and become the person they want to be."

Management Mentors define it as: "Mentoring is most often defined as a professional relationship in which an experienced person [the mentor] assists another [the mentee] in developing specific skills and knowledge that will enhance the less-experienced person's professional and personal growth."

Although stated differently in each definition, the common thread is that mentoring, or being mentored, is about the personal development of the mentee and is brought about through a relationship or partnership based on mutual trust and respect between two or more people intending to empower the mentee to progress in their chosen field.

Being mentored is like receiving counseling. Your mentor looks to create transformational change in both your professional and personal development as a business owner.

The History of Mentoring

The word mentor first appears in Homer's epic poem The Odyssey in which Ulysses, off to join the Trojan War, leaves the care of his household and development of his son Telemachus to his trusted friend Mentor. This turns out to be a bad choice as Mentor achieves neither. But not all is lost for Telemachus. As so often happens, there is a woman behind the scenes, a goddess in this instance— Pallas Athene [the goddess of war and wisdom].

Athene appears to Telemachus in a variety of both human and animal forms [twice as Mentor himself] and it is in the form of Mentor she is portrayed as a wise and trusted adviser and counselor thus helping Telemachus to grow in experience, maturity and courage.

It appears though that the word didn't feature in the English language until the publication in 1750 of the book *Les Aventures de Télémaque* [a continuation of The Odyssey], by the French writer Fénelon, in which Mentor was the main character. Fénelon's book became the most reprinted book of the 18th century, leading to the word 'mentor' being resurrected after a gap of three millennia. According to Andy Roberts [*Homer's Mentor - Duties Fulfilled or*

Misconstrued, 1999], the true Mentor was created by Fenelon, not Homer, and exists in Les Adventures de Telemaque, not in The Odyssey.

Forms or types of mentoring

"I am not a teacher, but an awakener." —
Robert Frost

There are various "types" of mentoring but for the purpose of this book, I will discuss 3 variations which are the most common that you, as a business owner, are likely to encounter.

The first is what I refer to as the **Ghost Mentor** *[also known as Casual Mentoring]*.

I have several of these "ghost" experts on my list but allow me to quote one example—Sir Richard Branson. Since reading his autobiography, I have been an ardent student of his business techniques and strategies, and I make a point of trying to stay up to date with his career and read any blog posts, articles or other publications that he writes. I even have his name on my Google Alerts.

The thing is, Sir Richard doesn't even know I exist!

We all have had this type of mentor or personal idol at some time in our lives, whether as a young sports person or a wannabe artist. They have indirectly affected our life's decision-making processes and thoughts and come and go as we mature, or our career or personal interests change. They unwittingly have or have had a major influence on our lives.

Although social media allows us direct contact with our Ghost Mentors, the relationship is not ideal. You are probably one of thousands of followers that have either commented on or "liked" a post. Unfortunately, that is about as far as it will go. This is not true mentoring; as you will have noticed from the definitions above, mentoring and being mentored is an interactive relationship between two individuals.

Although there is much to be learned from these knowledgeable and talented folks it is a bit like trying to learn a foreign language from a book—possible but difficult and likely to leave you more confused than when you started out.

The second category or type of mentoring is **Informal Mentoring**.

This form of mentoring comes about when there is a bond or chemistry created between two people who may or may not know each other to begin with. There is no intention to form a mentoring relationship at the outset but a common interest or shared goals will establish a link which will in turn become a situation of one person becoming the teacher and the other the student.

This comes about when someone, a friend or family member, a colleague or supervisor, or maybe even a religious guide, offer to help you resolve a specific problem. It may also come about through network contacts or even a casual acquaintance arising from a discussion at a business seminar with a complete stranger who subsequently invites you contact to them should you need help in your endeavors and actually responds to your inquiries at a later date.

This form of mentoring can be seen across a wide spectrum of activities, such as assisting struggling students to cope with examinations, support for troubled teens and providing career guidance.

My introduction to this form of mentoring came at a young age when I discovered that the thought of public speaking left me in a state of near hysteria - I considered 3 people to be the beginnings of an unruly mob.

Having shared this embarrassing fear with a senior manager I was offered the chance to shadow him while he researched, compiled, and presented his papers for his many public speaking engagements. Over a ten-month period he coached, cajoled and encouraged me through my first attempts at public speaking, and although I have never completely overcome the fear, I have learned how to manage it. At the time I had never heard of the word mentoring, but I have since come to understand that he was my first mentor.

There is no reason why short-term informal relationships cannot be formed, but do not confuse these "quick fixes" with coaching—more about the differences later.

The final type is ***formal mentoring***.

This form of relationship comes about through an individual making overtures to a potential mentor to establish a formal process in which a specific need is addressed, and an agreed outcome achieved.

These are structured relationships with specific outcomes agreed by both mentor and mentee and usually don't have a fixed end date. Let me share an example.

I decide to launch a home-based business but soon realize that I have little knowledge of how to go about developing a plan for the business. I accept that I need professional help but can't afford the luxury of a business consultant so I go looking for a mentor who has the knowledge and experience to help me. After approaching several possible mentors I reach an agreement with my ideal choice and we jointly develop a mentoring process to help me achieve my goal: develop a business plan that will help me launch a successful home-based business.

So, what makes this a formal mentoring relationship?

- I have identified a need—my inability to develop a suitable business plan to launch a successful business.

- To meet this need I have purposefully chosen to source a mentor as opposed to appointing a coach or consultant, my lack of finances being the main influence.

- I actively begin to make contact with potential mentors who I believe have the necessary experience to meet my needs, and several candidates are interviewed until I find a mentor I feel comfortable working with.

- A structured mentoring process is discussed, agreed, and documented. Both parties understand what I require and what I believe the eventual outcome will be.

- This outcome is not time based, i.e. to develop a business plan in 3 months. It is based on having developed a business plan that will help me successfully launch a business; even though it may take 3 months or even longer. The relationship will end once the new business is launched to my satisfaction.

Unless you are an exceptional "people person" with the ability to create a unique spin on why a total stranger should invest their time and effort into your endeavors establishing this form of relationship is a lot more difficult than most people imagine.

All of Part 3.2 is dedicated to helping you establish a formal relationship with a mentor.

Who are mentors and how can they help me?

> *"The delicate balance of mentoring someone is not creating them in your own image, but giving them the opportunity to create themselves."* — Steven Spielberg

Folks happy to share their expertize and life experiences with others are everywhere; you just need to keep your eyes and ears open to find them. But not everyone with a wealth of knowledge is prepared to mentor others.

There are those that specialize as mentors and make a full-time career out of it but often it is a friend or family member or a comember of your local chamber of business, a business leader in your industry or community, someone who presented a seminar you attended, an ex-professor at your college or even an ex-colleague.

Mentors are more than happy to share their knowledge and expertize with those willing to learn, with no anticipation of financial reward. They welcome challenges and will work tirelessly with the mentee to ensure his or her goals are attained.

If you Google "where do I find a mentor" you will probably end up with a list that will look something like this:

- Learning institutions: such as universities, colleges, research units, and foundations.

- Mentoring providers: there are many companies that offer mentoring services however many of them specialize in training in-company mentors, for example developing senior managers in a company to mentor peers and subordinates.

- Professional associations: examples would be an Association for Mechanical Engineers or Chartered Accountants or Marketing Professionals, etc.

- Business-related entities: this would include industry forums, your local Chamber of Business, formal business networks, etc.

- Industry professionals: these individuals are leaders within their own sphere of interest; Sir Richard Branson is an example. Approaching a high-profile individual asking him or her to mentor you will probably result in a negative response, not because they don't want to [my guess is they would if they could], but they are busy folks and simply don't have the time. Many do, however, provide indirect mentoring through books, training videos, website articles and other social media outlets.

- Friends, colleagues, family members, and former bosses: these are folks who know you and there are pros and cons to drawing on this pool of individuals, which is discussed below.

- Small business owners: personally, I have a small problem with this suggestion and the reason is that unless the individual is in a completely different industry and the help you need is not related to your specific market; I find it hard to believe that a business owner who could ultimately become a competitor to you will provide a positive influence in your business. Assuredly small business owners have a wealth of street smarts and personal experiences to offer and although I found most small business owners I know to be very forthcoming in allocating an hour or two to providing help from time to time, their ability or willingness to dedicate a large portion of their working hours to mentoring a new start-up was limited, which I totally understand.

Should you use a total stranger or someone you know?

There has been and will continue to be, substantial debate around whether to use a total stranger or rather someone you know. There are both positives and negatives to either choice.

Let's look at using a total stranger first. The obvious *advantage* is that they will call things as they see them, a crucial requirement if you need to get things fixed. It is pointless having a mentor afraid to ruffle your feathers and who persists in telling you what he or she thinks you want to hear. If you have a hurdle to overcome or a substantial adjustment to make in your business long-term projections, you need to know what to do or stop doing, no sugar coating!

Second, there is no baggage on either side, you are working with a clean slate which will allow you as the mentee to view suggestions and recommendations with an open mind.

The biggest *disadvantage* is the time it may take to foster a trusting relationship that is crucial in any mentoring partnership. This in turn will delay the start of the mentoring process. Some folks find it difficult to be open and honest with a total stranger, and this may lead to incomplete or inaccurate communication between the parties.

Using someone you know also has both advantages and disadvantages. There will be no need to spend time building the relationship but there is a tendency for friends, relatives or colleagues to avoid being confrontational, and may be less critical to avoid hurting your feelings.

What can a mentor do for you?

Being mentored can provide an individual with a powerful personal and business development tool which will provide a permanent platform from which to excel both in personal aspirations and achieving business goals.

The role of the mentor is to share their expertize, experience, and provide support as they work with the mentee to improve the overall performance of the business.

So how do you know if you need a mentor?

It is my humble opinion that ALL new small and home business start-ups should get the very best possible start for their new enterprise by working together with a start-up mentor. However, assuming that you have survived the dreaded first 12 to 18 months of business there are several indicators that may alert you to the need to think about getting outside help. And no, the need for a mentor is not confined to saving your business; in fact, many small business owners have used mentors to grow their company or to entrench sound business practices that will guarantee long-term survival.

Most of the folks I have mentored have hit a roadblock in their business venture and are looking for a way around or through the impediment. These roadblocks may stem from a lack of individual skill or trait or being inexperienced. This, in fact, may mean that the focus of the mentoring is on the owner rather than on the practices of the business, for example, the owner may wish to take the business down a new path but lacks the personal confidence needed to step out of their comfort zone.

Here are some examples of where mentors could play a role in assisting a business.

- Start-up mentor. They can be especially effective if it is your first venture into the world of the home or small business ownership.

- Strategic planning. Learning how to view your business from a strategic perspective and not only from the tactical day-to-day survival mode.

- Financial expertize. Most businesses fail because they run out of money, often due to poor financial planning and management.

- Improving your understanding of your company's competitive position in the market place and how it relates to customer management.

- Providing new impetus to launch a new product range or enter a new market.

- Identifying growth opportunities, product innovation, and potential new revenue streams.

- Enhance marketing and brand status.

- Your business is in trouble. Help is needed to stay afloat!

- Staff management. Not everyone is a people person, and you may need to get help with learning and implementing a more suitable and acceptable management style.

- Improving your self-confidence in your decision-making processes and developing a positive attitude towards your endeavors.

- Personal barriers. If you hate cold call selling like me, then you may need to learn how best to get around this problem. A mentor can also address other barriers related to your personal make-up, such as planning your day, prioritizing or keeping focused on the important issues.

What are the benefits of being mentored?

How you benefit from the process and what you get out of it is up to you, but the experts seem to agree that the advantages gleaned from a mentoring program are numerous.

- The opportunity to receive critical and constructive feedback in key areas, for example, communication, personnel management, and interaction, overall business skills and abilities, decision-making capabilities and crises management.

- Ability to help the owner identify skills and knowledge needs to achieve personal goals and provide "on-the-job training" in acquiring them.

- Provide the owner with ongoing access to a sympathetic listener with which to share frustrations, failures, and successes.

- Be able to enhances strategic business initiatives.

- Improve productivity.

- Assist with breaking down the "silo" mentality that comes from being "alone at the top" of the small business.

- Grant access to extensive expertize, practical experience, and wisdom gained by someone with many years at the "shaft face".

- Enhance professional development of the business owner.

- Set the foundation for creating a mentoring culture within the company.

Mentoring versus Other Forms of training

> *"The mediocre teacher tells. The good teacher explains. The superior teacher demonstrates. The great teacher inspires."*
> *- William Arthur Ward*

Why not a trainer?

The answer depends on what it is you are looking for in the way of help.

The problem with being a home business owner is that time is a valuable commodity and one you do not have an abundance of. As a business owner you need to be multi-skilled, often must take on tasks not related to the actual management of the business, you have little time for reflection, your learning curve is vertical and the stress and pressure of each day is high and constant. This makes it difficult to find the time to attend training courses or spend extended periods of time with external business consultants or coaches.

Being mentored is all about getting support, guidance, direction, recommendations, and suggestions while you go about managing your company. It's like using a GPS in your car. You're driving but there is the reassuring voice in the background providing relevant and usable information to ensure you arrive at your planned destination by the shortest and therefore most cost-effective route.

Each business owner has a unique style that the mentor should be able to identify and leverage. Being mentored is about "doing" while you are "learning" and that makes the mentoring style different to the classroom approach often applied by trainers and consultants. In all my years of being mentored both in business and as a corporate employee, mentors have never subjected me to long PowerPoint presentations, required me to read a 300-page document about how to make money [or the like], nor attend any lectures. It has always been about communicating face to face, telephonically, by Skype or by email with plenty of two-way discussions, exploring ideas and concepts and reporting back on progress, both good and bad.

Mentoring and Coaching -There are differences

There are definite differences between being mentored and employing the services of a Business Coach—note I use the word "employing" when referring to the Coach, a deliberate choice of phrase. Folks who are in the business of mentoring others do it because they have a genuine desire and passion to help others succeed. They also benefit from the relationship in that their own knowledge and/or expertize is enhanced each time they undertake a mentoring process. It is for these reasons that individual mentors do not charge for their services. I have used many mentors and have mentored several home and small business start-ups and I have never charged, nor been charged a cent.

Mentoring is more open-ended and sometimes less prescriptive in the deliverables. The mentor provides guidance, suggestions, recommendations, and insight, but you will do the work and so the pace at which you achieve your milestones is very much at your discretion.

On the other hand, Business Coaches are appointed to resolve a specific problem or provide training for a defined process, for example, I have used Business Coaches to help me develop a marketing pitch when releasing a new product. The agreement between the Coach and the business owner is detailed in its scope, has a start and completion date, a list of deliverables which are measurable, and the services are charged for.

If you need further reading on the topic, please visit **Management Mentors**. An excellent website worth visiting and subscribing to. Although they focus on in-company mentoring, they provide an easy-to-read overview of mentoring supported with FAQ's and PDF downloads on specific topics, including the 50 differences between mentoring and Business Coaching.

Even the best have been mentored

Just in case you were wondering whether being mentored is only for us ordinary folks, here is a list of some top entrepreneurs, entertainers and leaders who have all, at one time or another, been mentored or mentored others:

Brian Mulroney [former Prime Minister of Canada] mentor to Karl Péladeau [Quebecor CEO];

Marc Andreessen [multi-millionaire founder of Mosaic and Netscape] mentor to Mark Zuckerberg [billionaire founder of Facebook];

Warren Buffet [billionaire financier] mentor to Donald Graham [publisher, Washington Post] and Michael Lee-Chin [CEO, AIC];

Bobby Orr [Hall of Fame hockey player] mentor to Dr. Robert Thirsk [astronaut, physician, engineer, scientist];

Ingmar Bergman mentor to Woody Allen;

Joe Weider mentor to Arnold Schwarzenegger;

Richard Burton mentor to Sir Anthony Hopkins.

Now that you have an overview as to what mentoring and being mentored is all about it is time to move to Part 3.2 of this book which provides actual guidelines on how to identify your need, find a suitable mentor, prepare yourself and how to get the best from the process.

Part 3.2 - How to be Mentored

> *"There is nothing I like better than conversing with aged men. For I regard them as travelers who have gone a journey which I too may have to go, and of whom I ought to inquire whether the way is smooth and easy or rugged and difficult. Is life harder toward the end, or what report do you give it?"* — Plato

In this part of the Guide I will take you through the mechanism of identifying one or more prospective mentors, establishing contact with each of them, selection of your ideal mentor, managing the process and bringing the relationship to an amicable conclusion.

Remember, there is nothing in the rulebook which says you cannot have more than one mentor, however, if this is your first exposure to being mentored then I would recommend that you stick to one for the moment.

Understand why you need a mentor

Before you even think of contacting a potential mentor, it is vital that you have a clear understanding of WHY you feel you need a mentor. I have on occasions been contacted by small business owners with the question "I have heard about being mentored but I am not sure if I actually need one—how would I know?"

No, it is not a stupid question and if it was asked more frequently by struggling business owners, we may have fewer small businesses closing down in the first 12 to 18 months.

If you find yourself in this position, go back to Part 3.1 of this book and read the section **What can a mentor do for you?** If this does not answer your question here are some other tips to determine whether you need a mentor [or in fact it is a Business Coach that you need - refer to the section on Mentors and Business Coaches in Part 3.1 for an explanation of the differences in the services they each provide].

Do you have friends, relatives or associates who own their own small or home business? If so, talk to them about your predicament. The idea is to get a third person opinion whether external help is needed to resolve your problem and if possible what form, in their opinion, should this external help take?

If you know someone who is or has been mentored during their business career contact them and talk through the why and how they got involved with the process and what benefits, or otherwise were observed.

Go online and do some research. Pose the question to your social media business related groups or small business forums that you belong to. You are looking for feedback from business owners who have been there and experienced it. You never know, you may find not only an answer to your question but also the individual who offers to be your first mentor.

But let's assume you know that it is a mentor you need. The next step is to write down WHY you need help in two lines or fewer [if you can do this then you are very clear as to your needs]. If it is with your start-up that you need help, try to be specific as to which elements within the beginning process you need help with. For example, you know your product, but maybe you need help to develop the best way to brand it and launch it. The more precise you are, the easier it will be to find the right mentor.

List your own criteria for a relationship.

Many folks I have mentored have shared the opinion that being mentored is a very personal undertaking. Some felt that their space was being invaded or were asked to share thoughts and personal traits they felt embarrassed about. This is relevant when the mentor is a stranger to begin with. If you are going to invite a mentor into your inner sanctum, then you need to accept that to build a meaningful relationship you may well need to come clean from time to time. If admitting failure in an effort to get help is something your ego prohibits you from doing, then a mentor will not help you [or anyone else for that matter].

However, it is helpful to know at the outset where your boundaries are and what will be acceptable to you and what will not be. Draw up a list of your own criteria that will be accepted during the relationship.

Here are some thoughts on the topic.

- When is the best day/s or time of day for contact with the mentor? If you are out on the road providing a service to your customers, the only free time you may have is in the evening or on weekends. The mentor needs to know this up front.

- Are you prepared to share confidential information about yourself and your company? If you have a concern with product sensitive information such as recipes, patent designs, performance criteria, asking the mentor if he or she is prepared to sign a Non-Disclosure Agreement to protect your sensitive information is both acceptable and recommended.

- Can you accept constructive criticism? If you need something fixed in your business, then you must be able to accept corrective proposals or entertain new ideas and concepts with an open mind. Remember, the reason the mentor is on board is that they have "been there and done it" and it is that very real-life experience you want to learn from. There is no place for sensitivities in a mentoring relationship.

- If you operate your business from home, are you prepared to bring the mentor into your family space? This may sound trivial, but one of the most difficult aspects of any home-based business is the impact it has on the lives of the other members of the family, 24/7. So be sure that the family members are aware and understand why a total stranger may appear in the kitchen asking for directions to the toilet.

- Being mentored often means more work. You will need to find extra time to explore new concepts and ideas, evaluate changes, test outcomes in addition to spending time with the mentor. Be sure you and the family are comfortable with this.

- Consider the possibility that the mentor you decide upon may be a close friend or relative. Are you comfortable being mentored by someone you know or is working with a stranger more appealing? Some folks work better with strangers than with people who already know them. I know business owners who are more at ease telling a total stranger that their business is on the brink of disaster as opposed to sharing the news with their best buddy or family members.

The idea behind this exercise is to identify any personal or business barriers that will impede the mentoring process and if so, how you intend to manage them. Be honest with yourself and with the mentor. If you struggle to work with strangers or are not a people person, the mentor needs to know this and who knows, they may even help you overcome your inhibitions while improving your company's bottom line.

Preparing for the Process

"I am only one. But still I am one. I cannot do everything, but still I can do something. And because I cannot do everything, I will not refuse to do the something that I can do." - Edward Everett Hale.

As with any new undertaking, you need to make sure you are prepared and equipped to undertake the mentoring process.

Understand what it is you want the mentor to help you with. The mentor can't help if you are not clear in your own mind what it is you are hoping to achieve. Your ability to measure the eventual success of the mentoring process will only be possible if you can create a start point. For example, if you are looking to reduce your operating costs than you must have a clear, defined and quantifiable start position, i.e. my current total operating cost is xxx per annum.

Collate all the information you need to support your position. Using the operating cost problem example, prepare a detailed list of each of the cost components together with the relevant trends over a given period, e.g. component costs over the last 3 years.

If you have made any attempts to remedy the problem yourself, include all the information that applies to your efforts, even if unsuccessful. There is nothing more annoying to a mentor when making suggestions and recommendations for improvements then the mentee responding with "But I tried that last year, and it didn't work". Make sure you share this information at the outset.

What is it you would look for in a mentor? Must the mentor have owned a successful small or home business, or are you looking for someone with overall business skills and knowledge, one of which should relate to your needs? Do you find it easier to work with someone of your own gender or would you prefer someone of the opposite gender? Must the mentor be older than you? It sounds silly, but some folks find it difficult to learn from the younger generation.

Do you prefer to work with a local mentor or are you happy to find a mentor outside of your immediate vicinity? We will explore this choice in more detail later.

How will you compile your record keeping of the process?

Will you share your intentions to bring a mentor on board with your employees? This is an important issue. Nothing makes employees more nervous than change. Especially when they notice a stranger walking around the office and meeting with you behind closed doors. Employees will worry about their job security.

How do you intend to manage the additional workload that could emanate from the mentoring process? Are you able to allocate some of your existing workload to others, or reduce the time spent on less important tasks or will you need to put in extra hours over the weekends and in the evenings? If the last option is your only solution, then make sure the family knows what is coming.

The following are issues that you will need to discuss and agree with the mentor at your first meeting but list your preferences now.

- How best to measure progress? For example: using the operating cost problem, are you looking for a quick fix or are you prepared to look at the benefits over a longer period?

- Decide when it is the best time for you to meet, engage in telephonic and/or Skype discussions.

- How often should you provide the mentor with feedback?

- Is it necessary to flag milestones in the process? For example, should there be a quarterly review of your progress [over and above the regular discussions]?

- If you are in a fortunate position to meet with your mentor face to face, where should these meetings be held?

Finding and Deciding on a mentor

> *"Just about ANY personality trait or skill can be learned: simply find it in someone you know and copy it. Then watch what happens."*
> Steve Goodier

Generally, you will find a mentor in one of two ways—someone will offer to mentor you, or you will need to go out and find one, the most common method. Finding a suitable mentor is not an easy feat—despite what you may have read or heard. If you are not a people person by nature, this task will be even more uncomfortable. The image of emailing, or even worse calling a total stranger asking them to be your mentor will turn most folks cold so often it gets put on the back burner with potentially devastating outcomes.

Don't stress! There is a way to find a mentor that will not result in you having an emotional collapse.

This is important!

If your business is aimed at the local market than your mentor should be someone who is situated locally. Access to the mentor is easy, and they are able to impart their local knowledge. It is pointless being mentored by a "foreign" mentor who will have little understanding of the peculiarities of the market within which you trade. The only possible exception to this rule would be if you intend to enter foreign markets and need assistance, but in this instance I would recommend the use of import agents located in the country of destination.

OK, so by now you have decided on what it is you need help with and what kind of individual you feel comfortable working with. So, let's look at 4 ways to find a mentor that will meet your needs.

Note: There is no reason you cannot explore all 4 options, or more than 1, sequentially or together; however, I would recommend that Option 1-Referrals is a definite must.

If you need URGENT HELP, then options 1 and 2 are your best bet. Options 3 and 4 are more suited to circumstances where you have identified a need that may only arise sometime in the not too distant future.

Option 1 - Referrals

Ask everyone you know if they have been mentored, know of someone who has been mentored or if they have heard of a good mentor. Talk to those that have been down the road as a mentee. Get them to share their experiences highlighting the "what I would do differently" aspects. Ask them to rate their mentor and if they rate them highly enquire if they would be prepared to contact their mentor on your behalf and arrange a link up.

Approach your local Chamber of Commerce or Small Business Association and get agreement to advertise for a mentor through their publications.

Don't be shy about asking around. I know of a lady who stuck a note up on the local grocery store notice board which stated that she was opening a new florist shop and was looking for someone to help her with the start-up, but who would need to be prepared to do so for free. She got several responses within days and was eventually mentored by a retired businessman.

Option 2 - Using someone you know

Another option is to consider people you know who you believe have the skills and attributes to take your business forward. These need to be more than just casual acquaintances that you met at a business conference or seminar. They could include friends, family members, ex-colleagues and managers, close business associates, or academics you know. They would be folks you like and respect and have formed a working or social relationship with.

Advantages:
- getting the process started will be a lot easier and quicker;
- both mentor and mentee will not need to waste time assessing the other, they can work together on getting the problems resolved, or;
- if the relationship has been a close one in the past, the mentor may already know what is causing the problem and be able to move quickly to remedy the situation.

Disadvantages:
- the mentor may be reluctant to be ruthless when needed for fear of damaging the friendship;
- he or she might be inclined to say what they think you want to hear rather than the painful truth;
- should the mentorship go badly, it may destroy a lifelong friendship, or
- the mentee may be too self-conscious or reluctant to share personal or confidential information, which will hinder the mentor's ability to isolate and rectify the problems.

Draw up a list of people you know who might fulfil a mentoring role. Against each name jot down the reasons you think the individual will be suitable: this could include qualifications, practical experience, current occupation, and present location. Once completed scan through your list and eliminate those that your initial instinct tells you won't be suitable. For instance, you may have a friend that fits all the technical criteria, but you know from experience that you and he/she is like oil and water when it comes to business management styles. Similarly, you may have a self-imposed rule that says you will never work with relatives.

Assuming you haven't eliminated your entire list, you now need to evaluate each person on your short list. Think about your past interactions with each person, have they imparted gems of wisdom to you before, are they a good listener, how successful have they been in their own endeavours, and are they someone you respect and would be happy to learn from? And then decide:

- would you be happy to share confidential company and personal information with this person, and
- do they have the temperament that would allow you to work with them going forward?

Now you need to decide on whom to approach [hopefully there is more than one option] and it is time to contact your selections. As you already know the individuals, I would suggest that you either meet with them or at least contact them telephonically which will give your opening pitch a more personalized feel. Briefly describe what you are asking for and if they are agreeable to helping and if so it is time to formalize the relationship. I will discuss this approach in more detail later.

Option 3 - Look local

By local, I mean the immediate geographical area within which you live, or your company is situated. It could be your city, municipal area, state, county, province or even country [if you live in a relatively small country where inter-city travel is not a 2-day excursion].

Advantages:
- able to meet face to face as and when required;
- the mentor will be very familiar with the local trading conditions including statutes and by-laws;
- response time from the mentor to critical situations will be almost immediate, and
- there is unlikely to be any baggage attached on either side and the mentee may be more comfortable sharing personal or sensitive information with a stranger than someone they know.

Disadvantages:
- as the mentor will be a total stranger, the participants will need to begin the process by working on establishing a sound working relationship. This will delay getting to the mentoring phase;
- the mentee may be uncomfortable with sharing personal information with a stranger which could slow the process down, and
- it will take a while longer to find the most suitable mentor as opposed to using a friend or colleague.

Some suggestions to find a local mentor:

Use the Chamber of Commerce suggestion in the Referrals Option;

A good way to start is to approach the local business chamber or any business associations in your area and explain what you are looking for. Also contact companies in your area and have a chat with their Human Resources and/or Training managers and find out if they can offer any guidance as to how to locate a possible mentor in the area.

Look around your local community for success stories. These may be the local coffee shop you frequent, the baker, the grocery store, the municipal library, learning institutions or other small or home-based businesses in your area. When it comes to small businesses, you are looking for the exception; enterprises that really impress you as being well managed, customer orientated, deliver a top-grade product with reliable after-sales service, and performs in a way that has the local community salivating for more. The kind of solid reputation you want for your business.

List leaders in your community such as Academics, civil servants, religious leaders, Foundation managers or leading figures at your local Chamber of Commerce or Small Business Association.

Also talk to your friends, business associates, colleagues and other contacts in your network to get feedback on their opinions of star performers in your area and add their suggestions to your list.

Start the process by making a list (yes, another one) of the entities or community leaders that meet your criteria.

Once you have your short list, you need to begin making arrangements to meet with the individuals.

There are 2 reasons meeting with these individuals is essential.

First, remember you are dealing with a total stranger and you need to assess the person and be sure that they that have the skills and expertize to meet your needs and second, can you work with the individual or not?

If the community leader or business owner is not a total plank, it is very probable that they will have guessed that it is a mentor you are looking for and, may, in fact, offer to fulfil this role. Alternatively, they may explain that what you are looking for is beyond their expertise or that they don't have the time to focus on your needs. The odd person may abruptly end your inquiries with a condescending comment such as "sorry I can't help but feel free to contact me whenever"—to be read as "sorry, I don't have the time or inclination to babysit you". Although almost all the folks I have networked with for the sole intention of getting help have been more than willing to oblige, I have encountered the odd unpleasant exception, so be ready for it.

It is a natural reaction to assume that the best possible mentor is someone who currently owns their own small business, and you may be right, but there are several potential barriers to keep in mind. As you will very quickly discover small business owners are very busy folks and although they may be more than happy to grant you an hour or two to talk generally about their experiences, they may just not have the time or inclination to become your full-time mentor. Notwithstanding these obstacles it is still worth making contact.

- Visit them and spend time watching how they operate and try to identify what, in your opinion, makes them exceptional.

- Approach some of the employees and strike up a conversation about the business, an opener like "wow, you guys really focus on customer service", usually gets their attention, but be cautious with this process. You don't want to sound as though you are interrogating the poor employee, or you will get a very aggressive and negative response. You may want to use this technique at more than one prospective site.

- Don't be afraid to ask for an appointment to meet with the manager or owner—they will probably be very relieved once they realize that your intention is not to complain! When you do get to meet with them start off by explaining what it is you do (e.g. starting a new business, looking to expand, etc.) and that you have noticed that their company appears to demonstrate the practices that you believe would be ideal for your venture. Flattery is the name of the game but don't be patronizing. You are hoping to build a lasting and open relationship with the person so keep it honest and constructive.

- Ask questions related to their business and try to steer the discussion towards how they remedied problems or took corrective actions when confronted with situations similar to yours. You are trying to establish whether the individual has the skills and experience that would benefit your company.

I would also suggest that you avoid visiting companies that are or could be competitors to you. Your reception is likely to be anything but cordial.

Once you have done your rounds with prospective candidates, it is time to eliminate those that you feel cannot help. More about this process later.

Option 4 - The virtual mentor

The last option is to find a virtual mentor. This mentor is someone based in a country other than yours. Which is not a problem if, for example, you are looking for a mentor to assist you through a more personal development phase rather than a business-related issue where local knowledge is a factor. You may also be thinking of entering a foreign market and are looking for help although personally, I would probably use an import agent, Coach or consultant for this kind of help as opposed to a mentor.

Advantages:
- you can find innumerable candidates on the Internet, many of them are full-time mentors with very impressive CV's;
- you can find references for the individuals on their social media platforms or via industry forums, and;
- the mentee can contact a reference and get first-hand feedback as to the mentor's expertise and performance.

Disadvantages:
- no face-to-face meetings are likely to occur and you will probably correspond via telephone, email or Skype type connections;
- discussion sessions, particularly when formalizing the mentoring arrangement, may have to be time constrained due to these forms of communication;
- response times can be excessive because of geographical time differences between the mentor and the mentee;
- building close relationships when there is no physical face-to-face contact between the parties is difficult;
- a virtual mentor will have little or no knowledge of local trading conditions, and;
- this form of relationship can take longer than any of the others to establish due to the nature of the beast.

Suggestions on how to find a virtual mentor.

- As with all previous options look to your network of contacts first.

- Search the Internet but start with specific social media platforms such as Facebook, LinkedIn, YouTube, etc. Look for articles or videos about mentoring and follow up with the authors or links that they may point to.

- Ask around online Industry Forums that you are a member of. Post an inquiry on LinkedIn and ask your followers on Facebook if they can recommend mentors.

- Visit and subscribe to Business related sites such as All Business Editors, Entrepreneur, Forbes, Huffington Post and other similar sites that provide information on small businesses or publish guest articles by experts in this field. There will most certainly be articles by mentors or about mentoring. Short biographies about the author are often provided at the end of the guest articles which will provide links to websites, Facebook pages or other ways to contact them.

- There are several companies that offer mentoring support although many of them tend to focus on in-company mentoring. An example of this is Management Mentors.

The most important thing to remember here is that this form of mentoring will function around a long-distance relationship, which is not a bad thing, although it will take longer to set up and can be more difficult to manage.

The method for deciding on a virtual mentor is similar to finding a local one. You will need to locate a suitable target and then engage with them. Ask for references if needs be and contact the reference and get their opinions of the mentor. Because your intended mentor is "out there" it may be a tad more difficult to verify their credentials—but if in doubt move onto the next one.

So, you now have a list of individuals who, at first glance, appear to be able to meet your needs. Much like the local mentor search you now need to contact the person and establish a communication channel. Here is a suggested approach.

If the individual markets their expertise through a website, become a subscriber.
Take the time to read the posts and articles which appear on the site—get a clear understanding of where his or her strengths lie and how they would suit your needs.

If the person has written books on the subject buy them and read them. Extract elements from the posts, articles, and books that could help you in your business and try to implement them.

Open up the communication link by commenting on the website articles [or other social media platforms that they run], pose questions that may have arisen from reading the books or resulting from actions you have taken to implement some of their suggestions and recommendations, and establish a high profile as an interested and enthusiastic follower of his or her business style.

When you feel that the time is right pose problems and questions that relate specifically to your situation. When asking for suggestions at this early stage limit the approach to issues that can easily be resolved such as—what do you think of my website or do you think my payment cycle is too long? If the individual asks for remuneration before answering, then you are probably talking to a business Coach and not a mentor.

Implement the suggested remedies and provide feedback.

Continue in this vein until you feel comfortable to discuss the possibility of the person becoming your mentor.

If the person is agreeable, you then need to formalize the arrangement as discussed in more detail below.

There is no reason you cannot explore this approach with more than one prospect until you find the connection that is just right for you.

Elimination process

If you have more than one prospect on your list, you now need to start the elimination process—much like interviewing for your new housekeeper [I jest].

The best way to find out if you can work with someone is to meet with them [and this applies even when the prospect is someone you know] wherever possible even if that meeting is via a digital platform. Where the candidate is local, you will need to go visit them. It is not considered etiquette to insist on them appearing in your office on a given day at a given time armed with an updated CV, current photograph and a list of references.

If you have chosen a Virtual Mentor, this is not possible, so you will have to opt for the next best thing which is a Skype type connection.

Much like interviews with prospective employees one or two sessions with a prospect will not answer all your questions and assuage all your concerns. But you will get a first impression and may have to rely on your gut instinct when making the final decision.

Keep the meeting informal and explain what it is you are looking for in terms of help and what you would like to receive from a mentor. Provide a summary of your business and give a snapshot of what you are hoping to achieve from the mentorship. Don't age the poor individual by dumping a truckload of irrelevant information on them or blowing them out of the restaurant with a battleship size barrage of your problems. Keep it simple.

Ask them to give you an overview of their working career, how they got into mentoring, what mentoring projects they have taken on before and if the two of you were to work together how much time [not in hours, minutes and seconds] would they be able to dedicate to your project.

At an opportune moment try to steer the conversation towards more personal topics, for example tell them you have a family, or not and try a coax a little of who they are out of them without being too intrusive [asking them if they have a drinking problem when on their second glass of wine will not be constructive].

Two things to remember at this first introductory meeting.

Any acceptance by the mentor to enter into a formal arrangement with you is still only provisional. The mentor will most likely reserve final commitment until you have had your first detailed session at which specifics of the project will be discussed and agreed upon.

And here's the kicker—the mentor will also interview you. He or she needs to get a warm, fuzzy feeling that you are genuine in your wish to be mentored [and not looking for some free, quick fix answer], that you are someone they can work with and forming a long-term relationship is a realistic probability. They also need to have clarity that you at least have the will and determination to succeed in your business even though you may lack the requisite skills and expertise now.

If after meeting [or your Skype conversation] with a prospect and you feel that he or she is not what you are looking for—politely thank them for their time and try to give a valid reason you don't think the relationship would work [either at the meeting or at a later stage when you have considered all your options—not by email or text message please unless he or she is a virtual contact]. This can be difficult if it is just a gut feeling that this is not the right fit. If it is a gut feeling, you will need to get creative with your reason for not pursuing the discussions without sounding patronizing.

Now that you have found the mentor that is the best fit for your personal and business needs, and they have agreed to mentor you and are prepared to formalize the arrangement, it is time to get the process documented and agreed.

Formalising the Arrangement

"What I need is someone who will make me do what I can." ~ Ralph Waldo Emerson

Arrange to meet to discuss the process that will be followed. Ideally, you want to be looking at the first 3-6 months of the mentorship. This will allow sufficient time for the identification, implementation, and outcome assessment of recommendations.

If you have met with your mentor, then this will be an easy next step in your venture. However, if this is to be your first face to face, it can be a bit intimidating so ensure you have all your ducks in a row before the session.

Where should you meet? As this will be an intense meeting and concentration is the primary requirement, avoid public places such as coffee shops, restaurants, clubs, places of business, etc. Find a quiet, neutral venue acceptable to both of you. I have used reading rooms at libraries [arrange with the staff beforehand as you want exclusivity for the room], rented small meeting rooms at hotels and airports [where the mentor or mentee is in another city] or if your mentor operates in your neighborhood, either of your homes. I have even had a session in a park next to a lake—very relaxing, but almost to the point of being distracting.

Do your homework. Arrive at the meeting well prepared [and on time] with all relevant documentation that you may wish to share with the mentor or to support why you need his or her help. If you have been communicating in the past, the mentor should already have a reasonable understanding as to his or her perceived role in your business and how best in their opinion, they will add value to your endeavors.

How long should the first session take? Not a question easily answered. It will depend on the size of your company, the complexity of the help you need, and the mentor's time constraints. Whether you meet face to face or have to correspond by email or via Skype will also be a determinant. If you are communicating via email or Skype, it may be necessary to slice the initial "first session" into manageable chunks - 8-hour Skype sessions or six-page emails is just not an option when initiating the relationship. Compile a proposed agenda and share it with the mentor beforehand and agree how best to fulfil the tasks you believe are essential to kick-start the process.

Note: If you are using Skype as a method of communication it may be opportune to limit the first session to about 30 minutes and use it to agree on an agenda for the next, and future, sessions and agree on a how long each session should be.

Let's use an example to illustrate an indicative first session which will include some main points that both parties will need to discuss and agree upon [you will have already shared some of them in your introductory session but share it again, in more detail].

- Why you need a mentor—what do you hope to achieve through the mentoring process. As explained earlier, you must be clear what it is you need help with.

- Begin the session with an overview of why you believe you need mentoring—for example, *I believe my business is now at the stage that expansion has become a necessity to avoid becoming stagnant. I am not sure how best to go about this and need help to identify the best opportunities out there and have someone to guide me through the expansion process.*

- Follow this up with a detailed description of what your company is about and the current state of your business, e.g. doing well, about to expire, treading water, etc. Explain how the business got started, a description of the product/s or service/s that are offered, current market penetration, any growth patterns to date, the successes and failures and what it is you want to achieve going forward, for example, you may have an exit strategy, or you have a growth ceiling, you don't want to operate outside your immediate geographical area, etc.

- Talk about yourself; your background, expertise, why you started your own business and other personal related information.

Support this initial briefing with copies of your Business Plan, marketing strategy, financial reports and statements, and staff organogram if relevant and any other documents you believe will be pertinent.

Remember, you have asked this person for help, don't restrict his or her input by being selective in what you share. The more the mentor understands about YOU and your business the sooner help will be forthcoming. You are trying to build a relationship that is durable and openness and trust, on both sides, is essential from the outset. Keep the discussion as informal as possible—this is not the time to demonstrate your corporate presentation skills but by the same token be professional. Present the information in a logical and understandable format—don't be a grasshopper and hop around from a point to an unrelated point.

And please, if you have, shall we say, some unusual personal traits that could impact the relationship, share them with the mentor. As a mentor I have found it so useful when the mentee pointed out that they, for example, are sticklers for detail, fanatical about timekeeping, perfectionists, panic a bit when under pressure or have other priorities that will supersede the business such as family commitments.

Define the role of the mentor. This may, at first glance appear to be obvious—give me lots of help and solve my problem! A destination at which you will arrive but the HOW you will get there is an important step-by-step journey that must be documented. This is crucial for the mentor.

As a mentor, I present a rough draft at the first meeting in which I lay out what I see my role as and my understanding of what the mentee is trying to achieve—these need to be aligned with the mentee's perceptions. If you as the mentee do not receive this form of clarification, ask for it in writing. There must be total synergy as to what you want out of the relationship and what the mentor will provide.

Lets role play for a moment:

Mentee: My business has become stagnant and I need to grow either into new markets and/or with new products.

Mentor: I have experience working with companies in your industry and have specific skills and knowledge which will help you identify and take advantage of the best opportunities for you to grow your business giving consideration to your current experience, expertize, market presence, and product range.

Although the mentee, in this example, is making an assumption that the best way to grow the business is to either enter new markets or produce new products, the mentor is suggesting a broader approach; that there may be growth opportunities without having to enter a new market or develop a new product, although these options are not excluded. Both parties must understand what is wanted and what is offered. If the mentee is adamant about expanding through new markets or new products, the mentor will need to confine the tutorship to those 2 elements. Logic dictates that the mentee should be open to all suggestions and avoid being too specific, but I have worked with specifically minded individuals and so each to their own.

The mentor is likely to ask a lot of questions or perhaps request information that you may not immediately have to hand. If you don't know the answer to a question say so, don't try to bluff your way through. If a specific document is called for and you don't have it [you may not use a formal production schedule and rely on the whiteboard in your office to map out your production runs], explain why.

I must confess that as a mentee I have, occasionally, come away from a first meeting feeling a little bruised and deflated. This stemmed either from not preparing or having been exposed to a few truths about my business that gave the ego a serious slap. If this happens correct the shortfall in your preparedness by following up immediately with the missing or requested information and don't be afraid to apologize and learn from the experience.

As for the ego taking a knock—deal with it! It is very unlikely that the mentor is trying to humiliate you or flag you as failure—the playing field needs to be leveled and they need to have you understand that their role is to, amongst other offerings, point out where you are off track, why and how it can be remedied. All good stuff and learning to take constructive criticism and turn it into an opportunity does wonders for character building - trust me, I discovered this to be a fact, the hard way.

How the process will work

> *My best mentor is a mechanic - and he never left the sixth grade. By any competency measure, he doesn't have it. But the perspective he brings to me and my life is, bar none, the most helpful. - Brendon Burchard*

This is about the actual mechanics of how the two parties will interact on a pre-agreed schedule. For example:

- the mentor must understand how YOU would like to receive input; will you correspond on a pre-agreed schedule or only as required, will you need to meet each time or will telephonic or email communication be sufficient?

- YOU need to explain how you intend to take the input and implement it. For example, would you like to be taken to companies who have already implemented a similar change, will you pilot each recommendation before full implementation, and do you want the mentor present at each implementation?

- YOU will need to describe how you will provide feedback about the implementation and how corrective actions will be agreed and acted upon.

Note: Mentors have bucket loads of experience not only in their chosen career paths but also about mentorships. Draw on their experience and don't be afraid to let them guide you through this first session. It is likely that they will make suggestions or recommendations how best to proceed with the relationship.

After the meeting, compile a discussion document that incorporates everything that was discussed and agreed and send a copy to the mentor and get their agreement on the content.

During the mentoring process

So, what is likely to happen once the relationship gets going? Much and more [to borrow 2 well-used and very descriptive words from George R. R. Martin] but it depends on how receptive you are to suggestions and recommendations.

Continuing the above "first session" example.

The mentor is working with you to help you identify possible new opportunities to expand your existing business. After the initial meeting and a visit to your company, the mentor proposes to submit several ideas, suggestions, and recommendations within say 1 month.

You may decide you would like to meet with the mentor [if feasible] when the proposals are ready or have them emailed to you. The latter option allows you to digest what has been proposed in your own time, which may be the most suitable option given you need to assess what impact the proposals will have on the business.

Following your assessment, it is likely that you will need to discuss elements of the proposal with the mentor or clarify what is suggested. Depending on the complexity of the recommendations, it may be necessary to design and develop a detailed implementation strategy together with the mentor. This process can take months.

What I often suggest to mentees is that if possible slice the project into bite-sized chunks and take one element [a pilot simulation] of the proposed change and run it through your business. It allows for quicker implementation and it will highlight problems or bottlenecks giving you the opportunity to institute corrective measures whilst still in test mode. In addition, the potential impact on the business, if the proposed change is not viable, is minimal.

Note: The mentor is providing suggestions, recommendations, and ideas none of which are cast in concrete and none of which you must accept. There is nothing wrong in rejecting an idea or suggestion based on your evaluation and assessment that the outcome will probably be negative for the business. However, make sure you do your research before rejecting anything.

Having opted to accept one or more of the ideas or suggestions, it is now time to implement. No matter how trivial the intended change will be, draft an implementation strategy explaining how you intend to implement each stage of the change/s. This not only gives you a path to follow as you go about making the changes, but it also provides a reference to which you can return should you need to take corrective steps or need to deviate from the original idea during the process.

Allow the changes to run through your business and measure the impact. This exercise can take several days or months depending on the extent. Be sure to allow enough time for you to test the new concept in its entirety—no short cuts just because it appears to be having an immediate positive effect. Measure each change and determine the projected net effect on the bottom line over the length of your financial year. Implementing changes to attain short-term gains that could cause long-term losses is not a solution. It may also be necessary to assess the impact on peripheral areas; for example, will the intended change create problems for your suppliers?

Some things to remember when working with your mentor.

- ✓ If someone has told you that "you have an attitude"—lose it!

- ✓ Be courteous, professional and respectful at all times, even when you disagree or challenge an idea.

- ✓ Be on time for all meetings, take notes and be sure that the mentor receives copies and is in agreement with what was discussed and agreed.

- ✓ Provide feedback after each implementation—even if the results are negative.

- ✓ Be open to suggestions and new concepts and ideas. You may not agree with everything that is suggested but make sure your rejections are based on facts and not suppositions.

- ✓ Don't waste the mentor's time. You are there to learn and develop, ergo make the most of the opportunity. The mentor is providing his time and knowledge free—respect that.

- ✓ Don't be afraid to ask questions, no matter how trivial they may appear to you to be.

Enjoy the experience!

Ending the relationship

"The mind is not a vessel to be filled, but a fire to be kindled."
— Plutarch

How and when to end the relationship can depend on many things and could be a decision either you or the mentor take. I would suggest that some thought and discussion is put to this eventuality when you first meet. It is a touchy topic and talking about it up front helps break the ice when the time to terminate arrives.

Why would you end the relationship? There are several reasons, the main one being that the agreed milestones have been satisfactorily met and you feel comfortable enough to proceed on your own. If you feel that you have got all you can hope to get from the relationship, don't be afraid to call time. But do so in a professional and timely manner. Do not end the relationship with an email, text message or by leaving a voice message on his or her answering machine. Give the mentor prior warning that you believe the relationship has achieved its goals and that you intend to end it, for example, in a month or 2 months' time.

Set up a final get together [maybe over lunch or dinner or via Skype if your mentor is in another country] and share your experiences of the process with your mentor. Offer to write up a short reference explaining what you achieved through the relationship and how the mentor has helped improve your personal development or the growth of your company [mentors' value this form of feedback as it provides them with not only a sense of personal achievement but a point of reference should other mentees approach them].

I have read articles that recommend you make a tangible offer of a reward for their services, such as a gift or payment. My opinion is that as a mentor, I would probably be offended by an offer of payment. If I wanted payment for my knowledge and expertize, I would have said so at the beginning. I am also not big into gifts, but if you feel you would like to give a gift as a token of your appreciation, feel free to do so. What I have done in the past was to invite the mentor to the launch of a new product that they had been intimately involved with the development of. I made a point of highlighting his involvement at the product launch presentation and paid for his travel to, and accommodation at, the venue.

It is worth remembering that just because the current project has been successfully concluded you will never have a need for a mentor in the future. You have just spent months, if not longer, building up a meaningful and prosperous relationship with the mentor so asking to stay in touch and occasionally sharing your success with the mentor leaves the door open to call on their help again sometime in the future.

If you feel it necessary to end the relationship because it is no longer adding value, then my suggestion is that you proceed as follows.

Contact the mentor and ask for a meeting, face-to-face if possible. Gather all the information you need to support your impression that the relationship is not advancing your cause and discuss each element with the mentor. Again, be professional and courteous. The purpose of the meeting is to end the process positively. No mudslinging!

It is important for the mentor to understand what is causing the stagnation and you both need to explore whether there is a possibility of resurrecting the relationship. But if you feel that it has gone as far as it can, end it. Whether to provide a written reference is up to you but I ask that unless the mentor has turned out to be a complete ass [in which case you are free to terminate the process in any manner you see fit], the association is ended amicably.

It is possible that the mentor may need or choose to end the relationship prematurely. This could be for personal reasons or that he or she feels you are not upholding your end of the agreement and not making the most of their time. I hope that you never find yourself in this situation. If it happens, you will need to decide whether the mentor is correct and what you intend to do to remedy the situation or to take the criticism on the chin and bow out politely.

FOOTNOTE: THE POST MENTORING PHASE

The first feeling will probably be one of abandonment—help! Relax, one strength I have always been able to extract from a mentoring experience is a boost in self-confidence, the ability to take on the worst that can be thrown at me. I have a feeling that once you accept that it is time to move on, you will experience a similar emotion.

What I recommend that you do in the post mentoring phase is to either create or become part of what I call peer groups. This is about finding folks who are also home or small business owners and forming discussion groups to share your experiences as entrepreneurs. The easiest way I have found to establishing these groups is either through the local Chamber of Commerce or by starting with people you know.

I recently came across similar something called **Mastermind Groups** [my apologies if I am outdated] which seem to offer the same collective information sharing platform and appear to be well structured and organized. If, like me, the subject is new to you then there is a plethora of videos on YouTube that may help.

In conclusion

The first thing to remember about mentoring is that it is not a painful experience that you have to undertake only when your business is on the brink of failure.

I have always found the exposure, either as the mentor or mentee, to be an exhilarating learning experience and one I have not hesitated to invoke in my entrepreneurial journey.

If you decide that a mentor is needed, be confident in your approach to the mentor. Use the process to expand your knowledge and expertize and glean everything you can while in the company of someone who has been there, done it, owns the T-shirt [probably several] and is dying to share it all with you and just you.

My very best wishes as you take the first step in taking your personal development and your company from being great to being phenomenal.

As mentioned previously these are my own recommendations on how to find and work with a mentor and it is not the only way. Don't be shy in researching the topic further to understand what it is you need to do to achieve your goals.

Launch Day

You are only days away from the launch of your new business. You have said your farewells at your previous employer and left without recriminations.

There is no nagging feeling in your gut and hence no need for antacid medication.

All your preparations are complete, the Plan for your Business has been tested and found to be sound and your loved ones understand what lies ahead and are just as excited about the new venture as you are, and your carefully chosen mentor is raring to get started.

One final suggestion from me.

Take a break.

That's right. Step back from the whole process and take several days off to do what helps you relax. Spend time with the family, go hiking or camping, get in some extra sleep but above all try to clear the mind.

You need to be fresh on day one so the more you can put all thoughts about the new business on the back burner for a short period, the better.

I sincerely hope you have found this Guide not only useful but also an enjoyable read.

As you prepare for the first day of your entrepreneurial journey, allow me to leave you with these 3 quotes:

"The critical ingredient is getting off your butt and doing something. It's as simple as that. A lot of people have ideas, but there are few who decide to do something about them now. Not tomorrow. Not next week. But today. The true entrepreneur is a doer, not a dreamer." –Nolan Bushnell, Entrepreneur

"Chase the vision, not the money, the money will end up following you." — Tony Hsieh, Zappos CEO

"Always deliver more than expected." — Larry Page, Google co-founder

If you believe I may be of assistance in your venture or you have questions or require elucidation on any aspect discussed in this guide or wish to highlight topics or aspects of business ownership that you believe could be included in the book that would help future readers, please do not hesitate to contact me at **akanthony101@gmail.com**

If you have enjoyed this book and found it useful in your endeavors as a budding home-based business owner I would be most grateful if you would leave a review on the site from which you purchased it.

Johannesburg
South Africa
October 2019

www.ingramcontent.com/pod-product-compliance
Lightning Source LLC
Chambersburg PA
CBHW060827220526
45466CB00003B/1007